About the Author

J.D. Strazz started his first company in 1980, followed by two more, one in 1986 and another in 1990. Under his guidance, those companies were consistently rated in the top five percent in their respective industries. Before 1980, Mr. Strazz worked for a New York-based holding company. He worked his way up through Plant Management, Sales Engineering, and Marketing to CEO and finally as Group Vice President.

The Mistakes Managers Make and How Much it Costs Them

J. D. Strazz

The Mistakes Managers Make and How Much it Costs Them

Olympia Publishers
London

www.olympiapublishers.com
OLYMPIA PAPERBACK EDITION

A CIP catalogue record for this title is
available from the British Library.

ISBN: 978-1-80439-592-9

This is a work of fiction.
Names, characters, places and incidents originate from the writer's
imagination. Any resemblance to actual persons, living or dead, is
purely coincidental.

First Published in 2023

Olympia Publishers
Tallis House
2 Tallis Street
London
EC4Y 0AB

Printed in Great Britain

Dedication

I dedicate this book to my wife, Renate.

Acknowledgements

Thank you to Gretchen for encouraging me to write this book and to my dear friends Alex, Andrea and Michael for all their good advice.

Chapter One

The Coach's Brother-In-Law

First, I want to say that basketball was a big deal at the high school I attended. Everyone wanted to be on the varsity team, and tryouts were very competitive. Cross country preceded basketball season, and I ran cross country primarily to be in great shape for the start of basketball. Suffice it to say that I made many sacrifices to make the team.

When I was a junior, I played on the varsity team. I was the point guard; I was the sixth man on the team compared to being one of the starting five. I never started at the beginning of the game, but barely a minute would go by, and I went to replace the starting guard. I asked why I was not on the starting five, and the coach explained that the other guard was a senior, so he started the game. The honor of starting the game should be based on merit, not the year of graduation.

Halfway through the season, the varsity team had a record of eight wins and one loss. The junior varsity team had the reverse record, one win and eight losses. The coach of the JV team was the brother-in-law of the head coach and was about to lose his job.

The head coach called me into his office and asked me to step down to the JV team to help them win. I would only be allowed to play four quarters on any one night, so if I had to play all four quarters for the JV team, I would not be able to play on

11

the varsity team.

Coach asked me to think about it and give the Coach my decision before practice that day. I thought about how unfair it was to not be on the starting team just because the other guard was a senior. It was apparent that I was better at that position than he was. Adding to that unfairness was the expectation that I should be the one to sacrifice to save the brother-in-law's job.

My answer was to quit the team, and no one had ever quit the team before. The varsity team went on to win only two games the rest of the season. I went on to work after school and saved money for college.

Chapter Two

You're Making Too Much Money

After high school, I went to work in a factory that made rubber O rings. I was working two jobs to further add to my college fund. One job was working with a carpenter, and the other was working in the factory that made rubber O rings. The factory job was paid based on the number of O rings I produced. When I had created a product from five individual molds, that was called a "pass", and a pass paid twelve cents.

When I started, I could not earn very much because I needed both hands to pull out a mold, open it, load it, and close it again. The other obstacle was the molds were hot, and my fingertips were getting burned. It is pretty painful to put burned fingertips on hot steel. I asked other operators how they dealt with this, and they laughed and said, "Your fingers develop callouses in time." Well, I needed a job, and money, so I kept going until my fingers were calloused. As time passed, I developed the strength to open and close the molds with one arm. While completing one, I could open the next one. We were only allowed to work eight hours because the next shift needed to start at our quit time. I had decided to work through our two ten-minute breaks and lunch. I would put my lunch on a drum at the end of the line. When I reached the end of a pass, I would open a sandwich, then return to the start. When I got to the end of the line again, I would take a bite of the sandwich, repeat the process, and never stop the line.

To further improve productivity, I tried turning up the heat of the molds and turning down the time under pressure. My fellow operators were very unhappy with me. I was going to ruin it for everyone. I did not care if they were unhappy with me. I needed to make money!

Three weeks later, the plant manager came to our department and said I was making more passes than ever. I was making "too much money", so they were lowering the rate of pay per pass to ten cents. Reducing the rate of pay made no sense to me. I believed that the more I produced, the more money the company would make. Confronted with a decision by an authority that was very unfair to me, once again, I quit!

Chapter Three

"You Can Do Even Better"

After one full year, I had enough money for one year of college. Still, life intervened, and I needed money to help the family after an auto accident. So, I went to work full-time in a factory on the second shift and attended a local community college part-time during the day.

I never had much time for a social life; I was on a schedule that made it difficult. I was working six days a week. Luckily, I met a great lady, and we managed with phone calls during the week and saw each other on Sundays. We got engaged!

After eighteen months, I had moved my way up from the lowliest job in the factory to a good position in the machine shop. I enjoyed the work, so I took some home correspondence courses on "Machine Shop Tools and Equipment." Work wasn't so much like work when I liked what I was doing. I loved the precision that was required.

Unfortunately, there was a war at the time, and there was this thing called the DRAFT. I was drafted and spent the next two years in the United States Army. The army sent me sent to Track and Wheel School. I became a mechanic to provide maintenance on tanks, armored personnel carriers, trucks, and Jeeps. After serving my time, I was honorably discharged and ready to start my life again.

While in the army, I learned quite a bit about myself. I

15

realized I had some natural leadership skills, a very high mechanical aptitude, and that I could get along very well with just about anyone. I set my sights on learning a trade that involved precision work. Still, I also wanted to attend college part-time to study Business. I hoped that one day I would advance to a career in sales because I liked the idea of earning based on my performance rather than a manager's discretion.

That fall, I was accepted into an apprenticeship in tool and die making and married the wonderful woman waiting for me for what seemed like forever. I enrolled in a community college to take evening classes.

I was fortunate to be accepted into the apprenticeship program of a company with a reputation for being the best tool and die Shop east of the Mississippi. Many tool and die Shops produced dies for sale, and some ran production off the dies they had created in an area referred to as the Stamping department. The owner believed that this department was the best place for an apprentice to start, so that is where I was assigned.

The production supervisor introduced me to the person responsible for the press and die combination. The production super told me that the record number of parts produced in a single ten-hour shift was thirty-eight thousand. He then left me with the operator to teach me how to run the equipment. I felt fortunate to win this apprenticeship and did not want to lose it. I had been aware of how vital these early weeks and months would be, and even though I was starting at minimum wage, I wanted to beat that record! I will spare all the details of how over the next two weeks, I managed to keep this piece of equipment running when it would typically not be running. Still, after one week, I was very close to the record, and after two weeks, I produced forty-five thousand pieces in a ten-hour shift. Finally, one morning the production supervisor came in around nine o'clock.

He walked over to me with his cup of coffee and said, "I understand you broke the production record on this unit yesterday."

I said, "Yes, sir."

Then he said, "I always knew we could do that and probably do even better."

All I could say was, "Thank you, sir."

I thought to myself, am I ever going to work for a manager that isn't a jerk? The next couple of weeks, production went down below even the old record, so another visit by the supervisor.

"What's the problem with this unit? I see you are working just as hard as ever, but production is off."

I replied, "Quality control personnel keep stopping the press. Tool makers are required to solve the problem. Then again, something else goes wrong."

He said, "Those tool makers are going to hear from me."

Over the years, I have learned several lessons from being mismanaged. One, treat people fairly, or you will lose them. Two, offer praise when people deserve it. It will motivate them. Three, pay people based on performance; they should not have to ask for a raise. Four, production depends on the person performing the task. The person has to be self-motivated. If I ever become a manager, I will never demotivate an employee and do my best to create a positive attitude and morale. Why do so many managers do the opposite?

Chapter Four

Just Not Fair

Time in Grade. It was common in the military and the apprenticeship that receiving a pay increase on merit was impossible until a certain amount of time passed. In the apprentice program, a person starts at minimum wage and gets a raise every three months. At the end of four years, the apprentice graduates and is designated a journeyman and paid seventy percent of the scale set for journeymen.

I entered the apprenticeship with the advantage of the previous experience obtained working in a machine shop and my two years as a mechanic in the army. Another advantage was my fondness for geometry and trigonometry. It turned out that not that many journeymen were comfortable with the higher math requirements. The engineering departments primarily took care of the higher math requirements.

With my previous work experience and intense study of all classroom materials in the apprenticeship program, I was privileged to be trusted to build a progressive die during the second year of my apprenticeship. At the end of the apprenticeship, the state holds a competition. No need to go into the details of the competition; suffice it to say, it is a grueling eight-hour task. I finished third in the state of Ohio.

In my third and fourth year as an apprentice, I was building tools and realized I was better at it than some experienced journeymen. And yet I was being paid less than seventy percent of their base wage. I never asked for a raise and was not about to. Upon completing my apprenticeship, I started looking for a job and quickly found one. After being tested by my prospective employer, I received an offer of ten percent over the base wage for journeymen! That offer amounted to a forty percent pay increase. I tendered my resignation to my current employer. Shortly after that, the owner asked me to come to his office. The owner offered to raise my pay to the base rate, a thirty percent increase. To his surprise, my answer was, "No, thank you."

He asked me, "Why are you so determined to quit?"

I replied, "Because you have known, for the past two years, that I was worth thirty percent more, and you didn't pay me accordingly. You used the apprenticeship to take advantage of me. I want to be paid fairly! I don't want to work for someone that cheats me out of what I deserve."

Chapter Five

Promote From Within

I enjoyed working as a tool and die maker, but I continued to attend night school and still hoped to find a job in Industrial Sales. The people at the new company I was working at recognized my abilities, and I got along very well with everyone. A standard work week was ten hours a day and five hours on Saturday. The money I was making with overtime pay was enough that my wife and I saw our way clear to buy our first house. Working fifty-five hours a week and college nights didn't exactly leave a lot of time for fun and games, but my wife was right behind me in the willingness to sacrifice to get ahead. Sometime during the following year, the owner of the company asked me to come to his office. He asked me if I thought I could learn to engineer tools and do the estimating for the company. He was impressed with my corrections to designs and my math skills. In my mind, I said, "Thank you, God," but to the owner, I said, "That is why I have been going to college nights for four years." At this, he was surprised because no one there knew I was a part-time college student. He left it at, "Okay, I'll get back to you."

I asked my wife to type up a list of all the classes I completed, including the course description and the grades I received. I was constantly on the dean's list, and I can't remember ever getting anything below a B. When my wife completed preparing the list, I presented it to the owner's secretary and waited for a response.

Days turned into weeks, and weeks turned into a month. Finally, one-day construction started on an office in the main office area. The owner posted an announcement on the company bulletin board. A new estimator had been hired and would begin at the beginning of the month. The information included an introduction to the new estimator — which wasn't me! I inquired and was told by the owner that the person hired was an experienced estimator and would require very little training and that that was the reason for the owner's decision. I said I understood but immediately started looking for an Industrial Sales position. I asked myself, "Why is it so difficult to find a manager that treats people fairly?"

I was offered two positions in less than three weeks. One opportunity was with a company that produced traveling wire electrical discharge machines, and the other was with a company that made numerical controlled machining centers. In both companies, I would have to go through an in-house training program for twelve weeks before being assigned a territory. In both positions, the compensation package was a salary and a commission based on a percentage of the sales generated. I gave my supervisor notice the following Monday. The president's only comment was, "I should have kept my mouth shut."

I said, "No, I think you should have allowed me to prove myself."

Word of my departure spread through the local tool and die community as if there was a hotline connecting all tool and die and metal stamping companies. I received a call from a local company that had a stellar reputation. An offer was made and was accepted. I was to work in engineering to advance my knowledge of progressive die design. I also needed to become familiar with the formulas that this company used to calculate the selling price of tools and metal stampings. Once familiar, I would report to the sales manager and receive a salary and commission compensation package.

Chapter Six

Lack of Ethics

At my new position, my first assignment was to work with the purchasing manager and learn about the purchase of raw materials required for the production of a tool and the raw material necessary to run the tool that will make the parts. Barely a few weeks passed when life intervened again! The plant manager came to me and explained that the production foreman had quit. They needed me to fill in until they could hire someone.

That next day I reported to the production area. Management had not posted an announcement, so I called a meeting and explained the situation. Once again, the student! I knew how to set a die but only to try it out to see if it would produce parts that met blueprint specifications. I knew nothing about how to set a die up for high volume production and little about all the various other pieces of equipment also required.

The company made money only when the equipment was running. So, anything that kept that from happening had to be eliminated or reduced. I asked a thousand questions and made observations regarding bottlenecks and frustrations on the part of the people working in the department. Oddly, many of my suggestions made the production workers happy, so they gladly embraced the changes. Production started running smoother, and the group accepted me for my knowledge and willingness to learn from them.

I could not help but notice that some of the people in the department were more diligent than others. No one knows better about an individual's work effort and performance than fellow workers. One individual stood out as one who was interested in doing as little as possible. I had to think about addressing him because this was my first attempt at criticizing an employee. One thing I had made clear to the plant manager when I accepted this position was that I had to have the authority to hire, fire, and negotiate wages. If I didn't have that authority, my being in charge was just a waste of time. The plant manager agreed, but he wanted me to discuss any move with him first. I didn't get to think about how to address this one individual for very long because one day he came up to me on the shop floor. He told me I had to give him a raise! He reasoned that he and his wife were expecting another child, and they "Just can't make it on what he is earning."

My response was, "I could not set wages based on the number of children someone decides to have. The decision to add to the family or any other expense is a personal choice for which you must be responsible. If your expenses exceed your income, that's on you and not my responsibility. I have been thinking about how to approach you with my opinion of your work effort, and it's not a favorable opinion. Your family is your responsibility, and you should consider how your performance has jeopardized your employment and what that would do to your family. I would suggest you start to earn what you are getting paid."

That individual improved his performance significantly, and everyone noticed that too. It was a real lesson for me because, after that little two-minute exchange, I saw an overall improvement in attitude and morale. It makes sense that if management lets a select few get by with poor performance, it's unfair to those performing at a higher level. That is a real demotivator.

The plant manager had been observing my alterations, some of which were outside the norm for a production foreman, but nothing was said. Some of my observations crossed the line between production, engineering, and purchasing. I felt the need to ask for approval from the plant manager to make those changes. Permission was granted, and I then presented my suggestions to the various departments. It was obvious that purchasing and engineering were operating in separate worlds before this point in time. I spent the next six months learning all about the equipment from the in-house maintenance crew and any factory authorized repair people that were brought in. I read manuals produced by the builders of any equipment used in production. I read manuals produced by raw material suppliers and interviewed salespeople proposing state-of-the-art equipment to replace existing equipment. The downside was that the management of the company was not looking to replace me, and I still wanted to get into sales. I wanted my compensation to be partially based on commissions because I believed I could sell!

I approached the company's president with a proposal to help train any new person to replace me and to be available if that person did not work out. It was agreed upon, except for one more request. This request was due to the opportunity to do business with two new customers, IBM and Xerox. The company's existing quality control program did not meet IBM and Xerox standards. I was handed their requirements and was tasked with getting their approval. Upon completion of that task, I would be assigned to the engineering department to learn to quote tools and stampings, and then I would be on the road to service house accounts and win new accounts.

One month later, I received approval from IBM and Xerox, and into the engineering department I went. All my previous experience paid off. In engineering I was tutored by one of the best tooling engineers in the business. Design and estimating were just so logical that they seemed easy, but only because of all the years spent working my way from the ground up.

Finally, sales! I was directed by the sales manager regarding any issues with house accounts, but I was on my own for sourcing and approaching new accounts. I was on fire; the house accounts, purchasing, and engineering departments were happy with me because, as a sales engineer, I could answer questions and give advice without referring to the home office. I could work with our customer's engineers and production people to resolve issues, many of which were their internal problems. Purchasing loved that I made their problems go away. It seems their factory supervisors had a universal inclination to blame suppliers for issues without spending much time on analysis. Blaming suppliers was a headache for purchasing, and I relieved them of this aggravation.

Having worked at several other companies before this one, I knew of many customers who would be considered new. I made my list, researched, and started making phone calls and appointments. My in-depth background had me head and shoulders ahead of so many other salespeople that it was not long before the orders came in. My commission was a percentage of the sale, and in no time I could do percentage calculations as fast as any calculator.

At some point, I asked the sales manager about the distribution of commission checks. He responded that they liked to let it accumulate until it was sizable rather than generate a lot of small checks. He had a different definition of sizable than I did, but that's okay. I considered it money in the bank.

After a reasonable period, I had *my* definition of sizable, so I went to the president and requested my commission disbursement. Unfortunately, the president had a much different number than I had! Many of the new accounts were, by him, considered house accounts because, over the past twenty-five years, they had either done business with them, called on them, or *mailed them a brochure*! He finished with he could never pay a salesman more than he was paying his plant manager (referring to my calculation). Shame on me for not getting a clear definition of house account in writing before busting my hump for the previous year. After two semesters of Business Law, I should have known better, but suffice it to say that this was the last time I ever let my enthusiasm get in the way of a contract! That next day I ran an ad in the Wall Street Journal stating my qualifications. Years later, I learned that the president of this company had a reputation for using this tactic as part of his growth strategy. When new accounts were established, he would dismiss the salesperson and designate the new accounts, just acquired, as house accounts. A lesson in ethics!

Chapter Seven

He Took Away Their Chairs

The Wall Street classified ad paid off, and I scheduled my first interview. The position was Assistant Sales Manager. This company did not have a sales staff; they instead used a network of manufactures representatives. The assistant sales manager was responsible for supporting the reps, quoting all inquiries, and processing any new purchase orders received. The sales manager interviewed me for about an hour, then asked if I had the time to meet with the president of the company. After the interview by the president, an offer was presented, which I accepted. That same day I tendered my resignation to the not-so-ethical president of the company for which I had been selling.

I started my new position the very following Monday. The sales manager was very personable and got along well with everyone. He knew very little on the technical front and depended on my knowledge in that area. The manufactures reps were happy that I was on board to support them in their quest to obtain new business and help them with any questions their customers had about any existing business.

When it came to processing new business, I would review the purchase order and make sure it compared to the estimate offered. I also checked the blueprints to verify that the prints that came in with the purchase order (PO) were identical to the prints used to create the estimate. I had only been on the job six weeks when a PO came in. I reviewed it and everything matched up perfectly, but in my opinion whoever quoted this job made a significant mistake. The quote fell significantly short of the cost of the process required. I knew it was essential to immediately contact the customer and confess to this mistake to give the customer a chance to place the business elsewhere or adjust the price. Time was critical, so I took the matter to the sales manager. He looked at the quote and said that the plant manager had quoted it. The sales manager stated he had confidence in the plant manager's ability to quote because he was a degreed engineer!

I told the sales manager I could not process this PO and requested we meet with the plant manager. The meeting took place with the president also in attendance. The plant manager assured everyone his estimate was valid and that he accepted responsibility for his work. The project was titled Timing Pointer. I processed the PO with a notation that the president and sales manager had approved it after a meeting on that date.

Everything was going well; I had established myself with the reps, the tool and die shop, the engineering department, and the customer service department. These areas were the primary areas where my responsibilities required interaction. I had been on the job for six months when I started receiving complaints from reps about the delivery of a particular item. I turned the call over to customer service and asked to be filled in. Customer service brought the issue up with the sales manager, and the sales manager brought it to the president. Several days later, I was called into a meeting with the president, the sales manager, and the plant manager. The company was in trouble with a significant customer because we could not produce a part called a timing pointer, at least not the way it was quoted. I suggested how it could be produced. The president accepted my suggestion, but

29

the company would lose money every time they made this product!

A few days later, I was promoted to Manager of the Engineering department and the Tool Room and awarded appropriate adjustments to my salary. My previous years of experience were paying off.

The downside to this promotion was that I was now required to attend daily meetings held by the plant manager. These meetings were held in his office and required the attendance of all department heads. The plant manager (PM) would have each department head present any problems or issues they were struggling with and then go on to the next person without offering any resolution of the matters raised. This meeting would go on for well over an hour mid-morning. It made no sense to me to take supervisors away from their departments during production to hear about their problems and not offer solutions or at least develop a plan! After the fifth meeting, I stopped going, which did not please the PM. He complained to the president, and the president called me into his office. I explained my reasoning and that my being away from my departments hindered productivity, and I imagined the same was true for every other department head. The president sat in on the next two meetings and decided to eliminate them. All other department heads were grateful and aware of how this came to be. Let's say I enjoyed a certain level of popularity!

I noticed that dealing with employee grievances took up a good part of the PM's day. On this particular day, something more was taking place. The employees of the company were represented by an international union that was very powerful. The company had approximately eighty pieces of production equipment, sixty of which would operate at any time. Each piece of equipment required an operator; typically, each operator had a chair. Today there was no grievance, instead, there was a work stoppage! The PM felt he could "get more out of the workers" by taking their chairs away. If they stood and operated, they would pay closer attention. He stayed after hours and had a few employees remain with him. They collected up all the chairs and threw them in scrap hoppers!

I was promoted to PM the next day!

Chapter Eight

"We Can't Take a Strike"

It didn't take long to realize that the place was in sad shape! I was now in charge of production, engineering, tooling, and shipping. I have to admit that I was second-guessing myself for having accepted a position with a company in such poor condition. On the other hand, the thought that entered my mind for the first time was, "If this place can make money, maybe it isn't as hard to be an owner as I thought it was."

What disturbed me most were the working conditions in the plant. The floor was dirty, the lighting was poor, and the equipment had been neglected. Worst of all, the people in the plant had a very negative attitude towards, well, just about everything. The place was dirty even though the company employed janitors responsible for cleaning. I wasn't sure where to start, but I thought if I were going to be in that plant, it would be clean. I noticed that people left trash lying around as if it was no big deal. When I asked about it, I was told, well, it was not their job. Cleaning was the responsibility of the janitors. There were not enough janitors to clean up, even if there were three times as many. So, I dismissed the janitors and hired them into the maintenance department. Their first job was to clean or replace all the fluorescent tubes and light fixtures. A task that had not been accomplished in many years. I ordered many trash barrels and had them distributed throughout the plant. I asked everyone to clean up after themselves, which was like having one-hundred and fifty part-time janitors.

Much to my surprise, I received a grievance. The complaint was that I asked people to do something that was not in their job description! This grievance accurately indicates the poor relationship between the workforce and management. I had read the contract and intended to honor every part of it. It had been negotiated and agreed to by the owner of not only this company but of five other companies, all held by his management corporation in New York. It was clearly stated in the contract that management could require employees to perform work at a pay classification below their pay rate but not above, so when I contested the grievance on the grounds of that clause and won, getting people to clean up after themselves was like dealing with teenagers.

There was one other atmosphere issue that I knew would be delicate. Many of the male workers had toolboxes and carts. Most of them had foldout photos that were taken from magazines. I felt this issue, added to the "clean up after yourself" issue, put me in a difficult position. I came up with the idea that I hoped would turn that around. I sent out notices to every employee's home address. The notice was an invitation to an open house on a Sunday one month away. "We will serve coffee, cakes, soft drinks, and hotdogs. There will be demonstrations in every department — come see what we do and how we do it, and the task your family member performs!" After that, all I had to do was provide cleaning supplies, and the foldout posters came down at the request of every person that had a child that was coming to see what mommy or daddy did at work. Not one grievance!

The clean-up project had been accomplished at little

expense. The result was an improvement in morale, and subsequently, productivity. The next big issue was the neglected equipment. There were frequent breakdowns and sometimes significant damage. I addressed this in a meeting with the maintenance department personnel. The session made me aware of a shortage of qualified people in this department and that the department had been previously denied the funds and personnel required. I was well aware of the manufacture's prescribed preventative maintenance programs and asked why these programs were not being performed. I knew that the programs not only paid for themselves but saved some significant expenses and added to profitability and reliability. So, I went to the president with a well-documented program, facts and figures included. I was told he would take it under advisement and discuss it with the owner. In the meantime, "Just do the best you can with what you have." The president's reaction did not make sense! I could not understand why any president would not spend X if it meant he would make two X, but I did not want to press too hard, so I left the facts and figures on his desk and went back to work.

The first shift started at seven a.m. I would arrive at six-thirty, do a little desk work and be on the floor at seven. It was as if people had just crawled out of bed—slow walking and seemingly in a fog. I know better than to agitate anyone in a bad mood, but I had to find a way to wake the plant up and not waste half an hour every morning to get it going. The head of purchasing was a marine (remember once a marine forever a marine), so I asked him to get me a record of a band playing the national anthem. Yes sir, he replied, and did so for as long as I worked with him. That following day at exactly seven a.m., I played a rousing edition of the national anthem over the loudspeaker and entered the plant. The people thought I was crazy! They were laughing and moving about as if they were awake. They asked if they could bring in records, and I told them I would take requests. Half the employees were ladies. They were starting the day by dancing in the aisles to the tunes that had been requested. I have to admit it was turning some part of work into fun!

Other changes were of a more technical nature. Changes that reduced noise cleaned the air and improved communication. One such change had to do with scheduling the equipment. Customer service would call the plant whenever a piece of equipment became available. Customer service would react to whatever customer complained the most and tell the plant what they wanted to produce next. The problem was that sometimes this would cause the company to incur premium freight charges to ship to a customer that had given adequate lead time but wasn't the squeaky wheel. For the first time, I started to feel overwhelmed. I had to revamp the entire production scheduling system, update the equipment with electronic monitoring equipment, paint all the equipment to meet safety standards, somehow start a preventive maintenance program and bring about improvements to the very air we breathe in the plant.

I had to have a meeting with the president!

The meeting started with the president explaining that a large program had been quoted and a large customer was considering awarding the program to our company. The customer had one request before issuing a purchase order. They wanted to meet the person assigned to this project as the Program Manager. I was to be picked up by one of the corporate aircraft tomorrow morning to meet with our customers' purchasing staff and convince them that I could shepherd their program through to completion. I was all prepared to persuade the president to allow me to hire additional personnel and budget the money to do all of the above. My life was always full of surprises!

I met with the customers' purchasing and engineering managers. They felt comfortable that I could manage their program. They issued a purchase order, and now I was responsible for developing a relationship with a significant division of an international automotive corporation. The project was significant, but I considered it to be uncomplicated. The only problem was that the reporting requirements were very time-consuming, and I had to travel for face-to-face meetings with Purchasing at every step of the way. The upside was that Corporate would send one of their planes to transport me as close to the doorstep as possible. I started to like private air travel.

During these project update meetings, Purchasing informed me that some of their engineers requested to consult with me on other projects. This customer's expertise was in plastics. They wanted my opinion on the design of metal parts that went into some of their assemblies. These consultations became relatively routine, and I developed a good relationship with many in the engineering department.

Life was hectic, and sixty-five-hour weeks for me became quite the norm. I was in at six-thirty and always stayed to ensure a smooth transition between the first and second shifts. I cleared my desk of paperwork and then left for home around seven. One evening, as I settled in to clear my desk, the president appeared in my doorway. He told me that he was about to embark on negotiations with the union, seeing as we were only a few months away from the contract expiration date. The union sent a new contract that had more than everything and the kitchen sink in it, so it was time to begin negotiations in earnest. He asked me if I would sit in on the negotiations with him, and of course, I said yes because this would be a whole new experience for me.

During the next three months, I learned that the company was at a significant disadvantage. A work stoppage for a company that was a sole source supplier to automotive giants would be an end-of-life experience. An international union had the power and the influence over the workforce to threaten a strike and make it stick. The negotiations were somewhat reasonable regarding wage increases for the employees. The proposed contract required additional holidays with pay and a more liberal vacation policy. The biggest problem was the charge to the company for health and welfare that the union demanded. The increase was substantial, and the union president would throw us out of his office if we even mentioned negotiating the health and welfare clause in the proposed contract. With a little effort, we discovered that the marketplace could provide the health and welfare benefits described in the contract for half the amount that the union was demanding from the company. The president decided that he had to agree to the new contract to avoid a strike. It was a contract that carried costs high above the competitive market. The big winner was the union!

When the new contract was enacted, the president started sharing all financial statements with me. It was obvious that the company was not doing well. We were not losing money, but we were making very little. It hardly made sense to take all the risks of doing business. I was doing all I could, but at least now I understood the reason for not approving some of my no-brainer requests. In less than two years, I went from assistant to Sales Manager to Plant Manager, and I enjoyed the experience and salary, but I didn't know how much longer it would last after this last contract. I was about to find out when the president informed me that he and I were invited up to New York to meet with the chairman of the board or, in other words, the owner of the corporation that now held seven divisions under its control!

A summary of that meeting went something like this: the decision was made to promote the president of our division to Corporate V.P. in acknowledgment of all his fine efforts over the past two years! (This just so happened to correspond with my arrival.) Also, the president recommended that I take over the division but with the sole purpose of wringing everything out of it by raising prices and cutting costs to the bone. We would lose business, lay off workers, and eventually sell off machinery, equipment, buildings, and land. The new contract just made it impossible to survive the competition. I was not to worry because I would still be working for the ex-president, and he would continue to *guide* me! When all was over, I would be able to work for one of the other divisions held by the corporation. It was obvious to me that the president was taking credit for everything I had done for the past two years! I was beginning to wonder if being a jerk was a prerequisite to being a businessman! The only thing I had to say was that I thought I could *save* the company, and I would like to have a chance to do so before raising prices. I was asked how I might accomplish this, and I said by renegotiating the contract. My comment was met with a smile, and I was told that I was young and that I didn't understand how unions worked and that they never give up anything they win. So, get us out of there so we can use all the capital we get out of it and put it somewhere where we earn a decent return on our investment (ROI).

That night I decided I was going to defy the instruction given by the chairman of the board and probably lose my job. All I could think about was two hundred families losing their breadwinners. My father lost his job when the economy was bad, and he was out of work for a long time. I know how that affected our family. I was not going to be the guy that announced a plant closing on Friday as we handed out final paychecks without giving the people a chance to save their jobs. Over the next two weeks, I put together a plan. I discussed it with my wife! She understood the risk involved and gave me the green light!

Chapter Nine

A Fist Full of Rice

I called a company meeting! Everyone gathered on the shop floor, and all the equipment was turned off, so it was eerily quiet. I shared the shutdown plan and explained that I was in defiance of the owner by having this meeting and that I could get fired. I explained that I knew I could not go back to the union and ask for concessions and that everyone here would not want to give up any of their new benefits in the new contract. I understood all that, but I was not going to execute a plan behind their backs. The fact is that the new contract is so expensive that the cost of it puts us in a position where we can't make enough money to justify staying in business. I told them I had seen a documentary about life in the Far East. One of the things the people ate there that would seem unusual to us is monkey brains. What intrigued me about this was the way they were able to catch monkeys. They put a small hole in one end of a coconut. They put a rope through that hole and tied a knot in it. They tied the other end of the rope to a tree. On the other end of the coconut, they made a hole large enough for a monkey to squeeze a hand into and then put a handful of rice inside. During the nighttime, a monkey would come down from a tree, put his hand inside the coconut, and grab the handful of rice. The monkey cannot retract his hand with a fist holding the rice. The following day a man picks up what appears to be a baseball bat and approaches the monkey. The monkey tries to run but can't because he is tied to the tree. The man walks up and hits the monkey while only at that last minute does the monkey let go of the rice, but too late. Monkey brains for dinner. Please do not think I am comparing us to monkeys. I am saying it's natural not to want to let go of what you have. If you hold on too long, it is too late!

I said that I know that some of you can go to the market and get a job pretty quick, but I also know that for many of you, that would be quite difficult. So, I have a suggestion, the union works for you, and its job is to protect your jobs. Only you can go back to the union and ask them to save your jobs by revising the existing contract. The revisions that make the most sense are changes that do not lessen your total annual income. In other words, you will make just as much money as you would make under the new contract. I would ask that you give up the following paid days off: one, to donate blood, two, your birthday, three, the anniversary of employment, four, the *my* day clause. Two weeks' vacation after you enter the union needs to be changed back to one week of paid vacation after one year and two weeks after three years. These cost savings would be significant, in that, on those days if you are working, you are producing products for sale and profit. On top of that, I do not have to add the cost of additional staff to cover for you while you take time off.

I said, I ask that you consider my suggestions and discuss them amongst yourselves. Please take a few days, and then select a spokesperson or group to let me know what you think! Thank you for your time! I will see you all tomorrow.

A group of four was selected, one lady and three men. In summary, they did not believe that the company was not making money. They wanted me to raise prices first before they gave up

41

anything. They did not trust pretty much anything a person in a white shirt and tie had to say. I had to be honest and tell them I did not blame them. I told them I would get back to them with a plan.

Bottom line, I did not think raising prices was a good idea. The buyers in the automotive and appliance industry are professionals and send inquiries out to many of our competitors. Price is not the only thing they look at, and often it is not that we have the lowest price but perhaps the best quality rating or offer the best service. It would not take much for them to sour on us and risk a future with a good customer. However, I said that what I would propose is that they would elect again amongst themselves two or three trusted people. I would arrange for this team of employees to join our manufacture representatives and visit a random selection of three customers. The team can approach the buyers of these companies and make presentations for a price increase. I would commit the entire salesforce to present price increases if they are successful when they report back to the workforce. I asked, do we have a deal?

The team went on their mission and returned and reported that they were basically told to leave. The team was shocked at how buyers reacted so negatively and now understood how competitive the pricing market was. Several times they were told that pennies mattered and that any increase would result in the wholesale movement of business to competitors. So, the workforce agreed that price increases were off the table. The best part of this experiment was that I gained a little credibility but not enough to answer the next major issue.

There was one thing that I noticed that was consistent. The workforce kept electing a lady they called Mom to represent them. She was a single lady with no children and took care of the younger members of the workforce by cooking and bringing in lunch for them. She had their best interest at heart. When Mom said it, they believed it. Mom presented the results of the price increase trip, and that put that approach to rest. After the presentation, she told me that the next big obstacle to anyone giving up anything in the contract was related to the company's profits. The people did not believe the company was not making a lot of money and thought that this whole shut down threat was just a way to make more money. She added that people were beginning to comment about the elected committees being influenced by me with bribes. I told Mom, whom I will refer to as Ronda, that I had been thinking about this and that I had a plan.

One week later, I shut the plant down between shifts and held a meeting. I started by passing out six Wall Street Journals. I asked that people work together to find what they thought was a good investment. The group that came up with the best investment would get the lunch of their choice from me. Nothing like a little competition and a free lunch as an incentive because they went right to work. While they were searching, I asked if anyone had money in a savings account. A few people raised their hands and reported earning interest in the two percent range. The people searching the WSJ came up with a four percent tax-free ad from some fund or other, but it required a minimum of a ten-thousand-dollar deposit. I was pleased and asked for a show of hands, "How many of you would take your money out of the bank at two percent and go for the four percent tax-free if you could?" Almost everyone raised their hand. I said, "At this point, you have revealed yourselves to be greedy capitalist businesspeople because you are not just interested in earning money on your *investment*, you are interested in maximizing your return on your investment. That is just being smart, so congratulations! ROI (return on investment) is a very important concept."

"Next, I will share the company's income statement with you. I know you will not believe me, so I offer you this. I will show you our earnings year to date precisely as it was reported to corporate headquarters. If I lied to Corporate, I would get fired, but that is not a concern of mine because I don't lie, but better than that, I offer you this. If each of you kicks in a few bucks, you can go to the phone book and hire an accountant to come and audit what I am presenting. If I do not pass that audit, I will quit, but before I quit, I will authorize a one-dollar-per-hour pay raise for every one of you. The contract calls for twenty-five cents, so I think that is a pretty good deal."

I presented a flip chart showing sales and breaking down all costs. Rather than use numbers in the hundreds of thousands, I presented the cost of each dollar of sales. For example, for every dollar of sales, forty cents went to pay for raw materials. I continued line by line for every cost the company incurs. The final result of this meeting was that the people were so surprised to see all the costs and how fast they added up. So many of the costs were things that were a surprise. Some people had even mistaken in their thinking that sales dollars were equal to profit. They just never thought about all the costs because all they ever heard about was sales. So, I subtracted costs from sales, and when we arrived at the bottom, there were only a few pennies left over. The truth is that the company is earning only a few pennies on every dollar of sales. If I multiplied those pennies times all the dollars in sales, that would result in the total profit the company earns in any given period. When I completed that multiplication, the dollar figure was substantial.

Everyone wanted to know then why the owner was

complaining. I explained that lastly, there is this sheet, which is called a balance sheet. "You see here the value of the assets of the company and the debt of the company. You subtract the debt from the value of the assets, and you have the *net* worth. Or, in other words, if the owner just picked up his marbles and went home after paying all debt, this is how much he could put in a bank or the four percent tax-free fund you found. If you take earnings for a year and divide it by net worth, you see that it's not that we are making money, it's that we are not making enough money.

"The owner can take his money and do much better than we do here. In fact, for the price of the WSJ and fifteen minutes of searching, anyone can do better than we do here. We are now back to square one. Hire the accounting firm and verify that I am telling the truth! I have a clear conscience now. If you do nothing, I will start to do my best to make the owner all the money I can until we can continue no further, and you all will have to find jobs elsewhere. I encourage you to go to the marketplace now and see if you can get a job that pays you what you earn here and gives you the same benefits package. I can assure you that you will not, so you will be giving these things up anyhow. I have done that research, and no one pays for birthdays, anniversary days, blood donation days, and "my days", whatever those are, let alone three weeks' vacation after two years. It's up to you to tell the union what you want to do. My conscience is clear. It is now in your hands."

Chapter Ten

The Leap of Faith

Ronda asked for a meeting which I granted. She explained that she believed me, but most people did not want to give up what they had and were still suspicious of being tricked. I told her that it was sad but that I understood. The tragedy is that so many families will suffer, and I could not avoid that from happening. I knew that the younger employees would be able to deal with it better because many do not have dependents or can go back and live with parents, but the other half to two-thirds of the workforce were in their late fifties/early sixties, and they would be the ones to suffer the most. I thanked her for her willingness to serve on the exploratory committees and wished her the best of luck. She told me that this would not be a problem if I had been in charge of the company from the beginning. I asked her what she meant, and she replied, "The reason the workers wanted so much in the contract was that they were treated so poorly before your arrival."

That following Friday, each department supervisor handed out layoff notices to cut their departments to the bone. I had to maximize the profit in whatever time I had left. I had to approve overtime and started shifting people from one department to another to meet production schedules. I received a grievance from a shop steward claiming I did not have the right to move people from one department to another. I won that argument because it was clearly stated in the contract that management had that authority. I picked marginally profitable products, repriced them, and made demands for price increases. We would then be instructed to move the tool to another source. When we did, I would publish that we lost another job and the number of labor hours lost with that job. Then lay people off accordingly. Not once or twice but a number of times, we had to say goodbye to hard-earned work and hard-working people. In a relatively rapid fashion, the company went from two-hundred employees to one hundred and fifty. Then Ronda asked for a meeting!

She told me that a small group of employees would meet the union president and ask for concessions. She wanted to know from me what specific concessions they should ask for from the union. They wanted to be sure that it was enough to save the company! I presented her with a piece of paper with one sentence "Just go back to the previous contract except the workforce keeps the new rate of pay!" She read it, smiled, and left.

The union said "No, this union goes forward, not back." The workforce reduction continued! Ronda requested another meeting! She tells me she is going to the Nation Labor Relations Board (NLRB) because the union is supposed to protect them, not cause them to lose their jobs! I tell her that, as I understand it, the NLRB has lawyers that she can talk to, and I know little to nothing about what they can do.

I am sitting at my desk, and the intercom rings, I answer it. "Sir, you better get down here, business agents have Ronda in a corner, and half the guys in the plant have picked up steel bars and wrenches. I think there is going to be a fight." It seemed that the workforce had the situation well in hand, but I did go to the area of concern. By the time I got there, the business agents were gone. It turns out Ronda had signed a petition for decertification of the union, and the NLRB was going to hold an election! Ronda was shaken but smiling because of the support she received from the workers.

I had to hire an attorney to advise me on what the company could and could not do or say. I can follow instructions, and I did. The next short period was tense and involved my having to appear at the union hall. It was an intimidating experience, but I considered it almost funny. The union president wanted me to do what I could to convince the people to go against the decertification. The president made it clear that it would be to my advantage! I thought it was rather humorous. The NLRB conducted an election and decertified the union! Here we were with no contract, agreed-upon benefits, or anything else. One can only imagine the amount of trust the workforce must have had in management to take that leap. I had to act fast, so we held a company meeting once again. I first let everyone know there would be no change to their pay rate. The holidays and vacation benefits would be as they were in the old contract. I also would contract with the same health care provider that the union used and that the benefits in health care would be as close to identical as possible. Also, I would ensure that the company set up a pension plan comparable to the one they had with the union.

As far as any other details, such as grievance procedures and periodic pay increases, I need a little time to develop a plan. I assure you we will agree democratically on that plan. It will result in fairness and competitiveness in the marketplace, so we don't have to worry about going out of business again.

Chapter Eleven

A Democratic Way

The post-decertification presentation was once again a companywide meeting. The first thing I said was that there were things I liked about having a union. My saying that seemed to surprise most people, but I went on. First, I liked having a contractual agreement that specifically stated the responsibilities on the part of the parties involved. I also liked the grievance procedure because it was an effective way of letting us know about problems; if we resolve problems, we are all better off from that point forward. I wouldn't say I liked the negotiations between management and the union with very little input from the people. I was not too fond of the once-a-year change in the pay rate. I think that is a long time to wait, especially for people who are improving rapidly. I proposed that we have another company meeting, and in that meeting, we go through the old union contract and see how many things were in there that the majority of us could agree to as part of a new agreement. That will get us pretty far down the road in a short period of time. I guess before that meeting, we should agree that we are going to go about this in a Democratic way, meaning the majority rules. So, if the majority agrees, we all agree to live with it! I think we are small enough to manage this, and in no time, we will have a document that we will refer to as a "Policy and Procedure Manual." I said that before that meeting, I would like to ask that you all spend a little time reviewing the old contract to prepare for the next meeting. I want to suggest that we establish the following ground rules:

1. The marketplace determines worth, not you or me. If we get out of line with our finest competitors, it is only a matter of time before the marketplace discovers that, and we start to go out of business again.

2. These negotiations are not a contest to see who can outsmart, deceive, or trick. That becomes so adversarial that it destroys trust.

3. We agree to negotiate in good faith. We will be honest.

4. We will try our best to be fair.

5. We will be reasonable because when it comes to rules, I steal a quote from a *Star Trek Next Generation* episode: "As long as rules are absolute, there can be no justice." We need rules to protect the owner and the workforce from abuse, but we also need judgement on a circumstance-by-circumstance base.

6. Lastly, we want to strive to be excellent as a supplier because if we are, our job security and our future will be assured.

I propose we take our first "majority rules" vote on the issues I presented today. "How about a show of hands?" I said. The results of the vote are almost unanimous. I will steal another quote from an Egyptian pharaoh: "So let it be written, so let it be done." (Laughter).

Chapter Twelve

Who Can Determine Worth

I called to order the meeting on the development of contract issues. We reviewed the old contract and quickly incorporated many items from that contract into the new Policy and Procedure Manual. The meeting became less than productive when we tried to discuss the compensation package. It was apparent that emotions were overriding logic and that there was no sense in arguing about the worth of any one group. Fair compensation was undoubtedly the single most crucial issue and had the most significant impact on attitude and morale, so we had to develop a better solution.

I reminded everyone that in our last meeting, we agreed that "The marketplace determines worth." If the owner would allow employees to decide their pay rate, can we all agree that the owner would be taken advantage of, and then we are on the road to going out of business again! The same is true for the owner. If we let the owner dictate wages, how comfortable would we be that, over time, ownership would not take advantage of us! So, what are we to do? I would suggest that we develop a summary job description for each position. Then we make up a committee of people to shop each job description in the marketplace. No one from management can be on this committee, and no one on the committee can shop their job description. The objective will be to see what it takes to hire a "highly qualified person" for that job description. The object is *not* to find the highest-paid person because someone may be paying too much. When we evaluate the results of each survey, we will be able to tell what it takes to try to hire someone for that job that is very qualified. The committee will be responsible for combining a report they will present to the entire company. The wages and salaries they offer will be established as the *high* rate of pay for any position. We will create a review system so a supervisor can compare each person to the highly qualified standard developed by the survey team. If you meet that standard, you receive that rate of pay. If you are unhappy with the high pay rate determined by the marketplace, you can be mad at the marketplace, not me. While conducting the survey, we may as well research the benefits, so we can put this entire issue to rest until we do another survey which I suggest we do once every year.

Let's have a show of hands to vote on the proposed method to determine the pay rate? The proposal passed with only one objection! Volunteers for the Wage and Salary Review Committee, please see me! Your work will take place on company time, and you will not be restricted in the sources you are allowed to use. I would suggest that the closer your sources are to the local area, the greater the validity of the information. We do not try to compete with California or New York wages! Try to allocate your time to minimize the negative impact on your day-to-day responsibilities. If you run into any problems, see me directly.

One month later, the committee asked to present to the company the findings of their extensive marketplace survey. It took a lot of hard work and meetings to share methods and techniques, but it was well worth it. I did not try to get them to change one number. They made their presentation and passed out copies, and the nice thing about it was if anyone questioned the results, they would have to address it with the committee. I was out of it. There were very few questions, and the committee handled all of the questions with impressive professionalism. After that meeting, we considered wages, benefits, and health and welfare resolved, which were all resolved amicably.

Chapter Thirteen

Boss

It is hard to describe the difference in the attitude and morale of everyone in the company. There were smiles on everyone's faces, and we would joke around and have fun, but we were all working hard; in fact, we were producing just as much as we were before the decertification but with a workforce reduced by twenty-five percent. I was amazed at how much of a difference it made in the relationship when people felt like they were being treated fairly! I was happy that productivity was up, but even more than that it was such a pleasure to work in an atmosphere of co-operation. To have a non-adversarial relationship between management and the people was like a breath of fresh air to a drowning man.

The results were noticed by the board of directors at corporate because I received a lovely letter congratulating me on such a surprising turn of events. In that letter, there was a reference to the changes that had occurred "since my arrival." I took the phrase "since my arrival" as recognition by corporate that the previous president had taken credit for my work.

Our customers also liked that they would not have to worry about work stoppages or strikes. Things were going so well that it scared me a little. I was waiting for the shoe to drop, and I did not have to wait very long. I came to work one early morning and was met with silence; a noisy factory is a good thing because that means machines are running. If equipment is running, we are making money. The first person to approach me was Ronda. She said, "Boss lost his daughter last night. She was sitting on the porch, and there was a drive-by shooting. She was only twelve years old!"

"Boss" was probably the most well-liked person in the company. He was always happy-go-lucky. He had a wonderful smile and was a big, strong, athletic man but soft-spoken and gentle. When I started working at the company, "Boss" would refer to me as "Boss Man," and I would say back, "You're the Boss," Ever since then, everyone just called him Boss, and he loved it!

For some reason, everyone expected me to be upset about production being at a standstill, but I just asked for everyone to come to our meeting area. Everyone knew what had happened, but I wanted to discuss what we would do about it. I asked that someone be responsible for telling us when the funeral would occur. If it were to be a two-day wake, I would post a schedule where half the workforce could leave early, with pay, on the first day and the other half the next day. I would make sure the company would send flowers, and I intended to pay my respects. Believe it or not, there was a question: "Are you going to do this every time someone loses a family member?" I thought for a moment and said, "I will do it every time an employee loses a twelve-year-old child to a drive-by shooting!"

The city promised to help with funeral expenses but never came through. When I learned that, I called corporate and received permission to pay the balance due to the funeral home. Boss came in a few days later and had a hard time thanking me. With tearful eyes and a choked-up voice, he said he would be back at work in a few days if that were all right. I said, "Boss, today we just started a new policy adding paid funeral leave, so take all that time, and if you need more time after that, I understand." Boss was back at work the following Monday! When I walked through the plant that morning, it was the first time people came to me to shake hands, and some ladies asked if they could hug me. They certainly appreciated the way the company handled this disaster!

Chapter Fourteen

"Human Resource Manager"

The company's financial performance was excellent by any standard. Of course, I wanted to keep it going that way, but I was concerned about how thin some of the other managers and I were spread. The company had many resources available, and not even a rock could miss the importance of a workforce with a positive attitude and morale toward the company. It would only be a matter of time for that to change unless it was managed on a full-time base by someone committed to upholding the policies and procedures.

I referred back to the union contract. I liked the grievance procedure that had been in the contract. It was a fact that any perceived violation of the contract had to be written and turned into the union. When a grievance was handed into the union, it was the responsibility of the business agents to resolve it in a meeting with management. My predecessor had at least four grievance meetings a week. Once I was in charge, there were very few complaints because I made managers abide by the contract. Oddly enough, it was mostly management that was, one way or another, in violation. So, once I solved that problem, there was little time wasted with grievance meetings with business agents. I needed a similar system, and I needed someone to manage it!

I was still the primary contact to our largest customer, and due to an extensive new program that customer was very time-consuming. I was investigating a "state of the art" computer system, working with accounting on establishing a Standard Cost System, which required significant changes in the estimating procedure, and working with engineering on the design of the new program. I needed help! Before this time, all I saw were ads run for "Personnel Manager." With a little research, it appeared that this position had the limited responsibility to screen new applicants and manage the health and welfare package. I felt accounting could handle health and welfare, and managers could screen new applicants better than anyone else. I needed a person of firm conviction who could stand up for "fair, honest, reasonable and striving for excellence." A person that management and employees could not easily manipulate. Someone that could hold the Policy and Procedure Agreement as if it were the Constitution of the United States and act like a member of the Supreme Court. I ran an ad for a "Human Resource Manager," a position I had never heard of before.

As if that were not enough in the way of required qualifications, I also wanted someone that could effectively teach classes. I was committed to presenting financial performance to the entire company. I introduced the return on investment, income statement, balance sheet, and money management classes. If new employees do not understand these management instruments, it could lead to nothing but trouble. We also had many "in house" training sessions on tooling and machine maintenance, engineering, and quality control, that sometimes showed evidence of lacking. Where was I going to find this person? Did someone like this even exist? The answer was yes!

It wasn't easy, but I hired a lady with a master's degree in Education. One of the best hires I have ever made! It was apparent to me that she was looking for a work environment like ours, and she took to it with hunger. She taught us to prepare a pre-test and a post-test for each class. Management never saw the pre-test. But the post-test was turned in to management at the end of each class. Another essential idea the new HR manager brought to the classroom was the need to demonstrate evidence of the need for education on the topic to be covered. All that was great, but even better was how she embraced P&P (Policy and Procedure). Her intelligence was evident, and her ability to communicate was excellent. She studied and observed every aspect of the company from her perspective. It was apparent she was committed! After about a month, she suggested adding HR (human resource) assistants: as HR director, she wanted one volunteer from each department to be designated HR assistant trained by her. The assistant would be responsible for communicating within the assigned department any decisions made by management and any complaints or suggestions for improvement to the HR director. This procedure was our form of the union business agents' function and a process that worked well. In as little as three months, I could trust the new HR director to the point of freeing me to spend more time on some critical issues that needed attention. Her primary responsibility would be monitoring attitude and morale because if it was positive, it made the difference between a winning team and just a team.

One thing I had set as a high priority to work on was the way we priced products. I had worked in several different companies that were in the same business. I noticed that each company seemed very successful in winning bids of a specific nature, but none of the companies won bids across a broad spectrum of products. I won't go into detail here, but I started to do some research and run some experiments on the results of various approaches to pricing. I wasn't getting very far, but then I came across an article in a trade magazine that shed light on the problem. I ran with the basic concept and took it even further. I contacted the article's author and reviewed the system, and I added to his work. He was delighted to have helped and asked me to put my work in writing. I did and presented him with my paper on "Pricing Manufactured Products." I also sent the report to the accounting firm employed by corporate headquarters. I received a call from a junior partner at the accounting firm. He asked if I would grant their consulting firm permission to use my pricing paper. Of course, I gave my permission and received a thank you from corporate headquarters. I then instructed Sales and Estimating to put the system to work, and the results were almost immediate. I mention it here because it caused me to be even further from the day-to-day happenings and more and more into managing the future business that was coming in the door.

The HR director brought to my attention a problem that she felt needed my attention. She reminded me that every four months, according to P&P, every employee has to be reviewed and that we have been doing that but not very effectively. I asked for specifics, and she had many. It was apparent this program needed a lot more sophistication. Major issues had to do with managers not meeting review dates because they were too busy to complete them. I thought, "Try telling someone you are too busy to pay attention to their pay rate and watch what happens to their attitude and morale."

Another problem was subjectivity; managers were stating opinions with little evidence to back up those opinions. Lastly, the reviews that managers gave primarily focused on problems or shortcomings. It was evident that we had to work on a plan to present to the people of the company.

One good thing we had was the information from the market

survey team, which included the rate of pay for someone determined to be highly qualified and a summary job description. I told the HR director if she could work out a review schedule and spread the reviews out so that each manager had only a reasonable number of reviews to give over one month. Each manager will get the review schedule. That should leave each manager with no excuse to miss a review date. Each manager will get reviewed after the one-month review period, and part of the manager's review will depend on that manager meeting the review schedule. I will go to work on the subjectivity problem, and we will meet one week from today. In the meantime, have your assistant HR people communicate that you have identified this problem and we are working on solutions so they can look forward to another company meeting!

One week later, we held a meeting. I acknowledged that the reviews were not happening on timely bases and as a solution to resolve this, the HR director has prepared a review schedule. The reviews are now spread out over a reasonable period so that each manager would have no problem presenting each review at the assigned time. Managers will be reviewed at the end of the review cycle, and part of their rating will depend on meeting their review schedule. I have been thinking about how we could significantly reduce the subjectivity of the review program. Subjectivity can be the beast that destroys the entire program. I want this resolve to be as democratic as possible. I have come up with two major categories that I would like you to consider.

One category is all the technical skills required. The other category is all those things that are considered personal responsibilities. The technical skills, to a large degree, can be tested and your score converted to points. I am confident that some technical skills are more important than others, so the idea will be to make up a list for each job description and put them in order of priority. I believe the Wage and Salary Survey Committee can be very helpful in this effort. They spent so much time searching for highly qualified people in each job description. Personal responsibilities will be pretty much the same for all employees. I can give you some of my thoughts just as a sample: I think it is vital for people to get along; you know how I feel about absenteeism and tardiness. Getting along with management is essential. One last suggestion would be following all safety rules. These are just suggestions; I want each job classification to meet and make up your lists, then turn them into HR, but before you do that, try to assign points to each requirement. The essential requirements get the most points, but each category has to add up to one-hundred points. Do your best and then the HR team and I will meet and see if we can bring the program together for your approval.

Several weeks later, each job classification submitted its work. The HR team and I met and were surprised at how long the list was for each category. It was apparent that the employees wanted us to know that they did many things for the pay they received. As we poured over the lists, we were able to combine many of the suggested tasks. An example would be emptying the wastepaper basket and putting tools away into "good housekeeping" or cleanliness and neatness. There is no doubt that we had a difficult task ahead of us, but in time we had a document ready to present to the entire workforce. We circulated the review point system documents three days before holding a company meeting to discuss and hopefully vote on the new review system. We met, and I was thrilled that everyone was pleased with the finished product. Every employee appreciated our effort and that we wanted to evaluate and pay them fairly! I could tell we hit a home run with this program because the employees invited me to the corner bar after work, where it was explained to me that I would be allowed to buy everyone a beer. Gladly!

The HR director recommended that each manager set up a file folder for each person in the department. During the review period, the manager should document events that would result in the awarding or losing of points at the review time. Both parties should sign this document. Taking the time to do this also served as an opportunity to discuss the event and result in continued improvement. The review period spanned four months, and we did not want to depend on any one person's memory. When it is time to review someone, it will be easier for the manager to assign points based on already agreed documentation. If a person received one-hundred points in each column, they would receive a high rate of pay no matter what rate of pay they were at currently. No one would be held back by any arbitrary date or for some specified time to pass since your last increase. You will get paid at a high level if you have performed at a high level. The reviewer will convert points earned and lost into dollars. Employees will know what you need to do to make more money. Then it's up to you. Managers must ask after the review: "What can I do to help you win the points you lost?" The company is willing to pay for any education required; we will pay for books, parking, cost of the course, one hundred percent of all costs if you get an A, eighty percent for a B, seventy percent for a C. Suppose it's a pass/fail class, one hundred percent if you pass. The manager must also ask, "What are your goals? How can we help you reach your goals?" and explain that the HR director is here to help guide you if your goals are in any way of service to this organization. You have to put in the time and effort after your work responsibilities.

This will be our review system because this company is here not just for the benefit of the owner, but it exists for the benefit of all of us. If we make it great, we reap the rewards, not to the degree that the owner does, but then again, we didn't put up millions of our hard-earned dollars and risk them to the point of *almost* failure.

Jump ahead one year, and our ROI (Return on Investment) was better than any other of the (now ten) divisions owned by the corporation.

Chapter Fifteen

Win-Win

The customer I was personally responsible for called and summoned me to headquarters. There was a new painting process that this customer approved at the lab level. This customer was anxious to have this process applied to many of the parts we produced. The problem was no one was currently approved to use this process on a production basis. I was asked, "How long will it take you to set up a paint line, get approved, and start production?" My first response to this request was six months which the customer immediately rejected. I requested forty-eight hours to come up with my best estimate, which was not good enough for the people in charge. They said "I don't want an estimate, I want a promise," to which I replied, "Well then I will need seventy-two hours," which finally received approval.

I reviewed the required specifications on the equipment necessary to apply this new process. I contacted new equipment suppliers, but lead times were out of the question. Purchasing assisted in finding used equipment suppliers, but that equipment would have to be modified. We asked the used equipment suppliers to include the cost of changing the equipment and give us their best delivery promise. I constructed a timeline from start to completion, called my customer, and shared my proposed timeline. Everyone was happy, but the phone call ended with a threat, something like, "Don't even think about missing that deadline!"

I made a big mistake! I never thought that corporate would not want to provide the funds necessary to start this operation. When I called corporate and reviewed the numbers, it wasn't the money that corporate objected to. It was a fact that the paint business involved the EPA (Environmental Protection Agency). The amount of business this operation would generate did not justify the risk involved with the production painting of metal parts. After a day or two of considerable worry, I called corporate again and asked permission to start the paint business independently. I received permission and a "Waiver of Conflict of Interest" from corporate. I hired someone to come to work for me, with the first responsibility being to lease some space, then purchase the equipment and supervise the installation. We contacted the EPA and received approval every step of the way. I was removed from the process of pricing products and would only receive a monthly financial statement. I contacted a lawyer and an accounting firm to oversee operations and audit all transactions. We received approval from the paint manufacturer, and we were in production one month before the deadline. My customer was pleased, and now I was a small business owner. My wife was very worried about us putting our life savings at risk, but she offered her support. Corporate was happy that I could continue to work for them and that I was able to satisfy our biggest customer.

Chapter Sixteen

"Go and Figure it Out"

I received a phone call from the administrative assistant to the Chairman of the Corporation. The admin assistant told me that a plane would pick me up tomorrow morning to bring me to New York for a meeting with the chairman and that several other people would attend.

"What's this about?" I asked, "and what do I need to bring?"

"Just yourself," was the answer.

I hate mysteries! I was greeted by one of the corporate vice-presidents when I arrived. We were ushered into the chairman's spacious office and sat opposite his desk. The chairman entered and started right in with a presentation. He explained that over time he had taken the corporation from the two divisions he inherited to the ten divisions that are the makeup of the corporation today. His last acquisition was ten times larger than the two divisions he inherited, and he wanted to grow even more significant.

His growth plan was not to add directly to the current ten divisions but to have the divisions broken up into groups and have each group make its acquisitions. He wanted me to head up one of the groups and to begin to structure a staff so that I could focus on acquisitions and mergers.

"Well, what do you think?"

"I know nothing about Mergers and Acquisitions," was my

reply.

"Well, go figure it out, but before that, let's go to lunch."

The chairman placed two additional divisions under my authority. Compared to the one I had been running, one was smaller, the other larger but size didn't matter, they were both in bad shape. How was I going to properly run three divisions, two of which needed extensive upgrades to almost everything! I had to hire highly qualified staff to free up more of my time.

I had to spend time at the other divisions to make a proper evaluation of the current staff and the machinery and equipment currently in operation.

One thing that made all this easier was corporate aircraft. Commercial travel would have meant hotel rooms and time spent waiting around in airports, canceled flights, and missed appointments. With private aircraft, I could fly into airports close to the divisions, spend a couple of days, and then jet off to one of the other divisions. One of the ways I used to help evaluate a division was to arrange visits with a sampling of the largest customers of that division. Customers were ready, willing, and able to provide an unbiased evaluation, compared to what I might get from a sales manager or a division president. The corporate aircraft also helped with the visits to potential acquisitions. I was often the only passenger so that I could sit up front with the pilot. I sat in the first officer's position and just listened in on the communications between the pilot and various control centers on the ground.

It didn't take long to realize that I had to add staff to my division and change staff at the other two new divisions. At first, I thought that, if applicable, I could introduce some of the programs we had already developed in my division. The presidents of the other divisions seemed to accept this approach, but it did not take me long to understand that their actions did not match their words. I hate deception and how difficult it can be to detect. My standard approach is to win people over to something new or different by offering a logical explanation, so it would seem evident that this new idea should be embraced. Sometimes emotions get in the way of logic, and emotions become resistance. I understood that I have very little skill as a psychologist and that even a skilled psychologist needs years to deal with behavioral problems. I did not have years to change the course of a ship (division) in trouble! The single most unpleasant part of supervision has to be terminating someone. I drew the strength necessary for this task from two places: fairness is one, and the other is to save all the other employees from losing their jobs. I never fired anyone without giving that person adequate time to make the necessary adjustments to warnings. I should qualify that with the fact that there are exceptions. Immediate termination was justified when it involved dishonesty, fighting, or the use of drugs or alcohol. Yet, even with the situations involving the use of drugs and or alcohol, there were exceptions. A person who joined an accredited program would have our support to get healthy. I considered these problems health issues, so I wanted to hold their jobs open when they could return. Many managers felt no obligation to help employees with drug and alcohol problems. Managers and the philosophies they embraced were many times obstacles to success. Managers cannot hide their true feelings toward the people that work for them, and that, ladies and gentlemen, meant that attitude and morale were never going to be very good. I often wondered what made so many managers think they were so *special*, so much better than anyone else. I asked myself if it started in the education system. If you get excellent grades, you get approved for admission to special universities, universities that only accept the top one percent. Then if you graduate at the top of your class, you can get accepted into a grad school, and they only take the very *best*, and then when you graduate from grad school, the corporations send limos to pick you up, and you get hired by the very best corporations. So, you start to believe you are *better* than most everyone, when in fact, you are better educated, but you are not a better human being than anyone else. If you think you are, you cannot be an effective manager, in my opinion. The problem then becomes trying to replace arrogant managers because most of the people you interview have been programmed the same way. Still, you can find a few *kind*, well-educated people with perseverance. Compared to fake, I came to refer to them as people who are *real*.

Chapter Seventeen

Once In a Lifetime!

I was responsible for, mergers, acquisitions, and turning around two divisions which defined my work life for the last couple of years. I figured out that the companies I would want to buy were not for sale. Working with my VP of Finance, we put together the profile of a company that fit as a proper acquisition and spent hours with several resources trying to find a decent match. When we did, we would send a letter, establish contact, sign a non-discloser agreement, and ask for information, and then if we got that far, we would structure an offer. It was kind of like fishing. Some days you wind up with a big fat nothing, which is why they don't call it catching.

After many months and some luck, we were with one company very far down the road in the process. The VP of finance was working out the buy-out plan. Corporate had to finance this deal because the three divisions I was in charge of were leveraged by corporate, which left us with inadequate finance resources. Corporate asked that we send everything on this deal to them. I sent everything and my VP of finance to corporate three days later.

After a couple of days at corporate, the news was that we had to pass on the deal. It wasn't a good deal, it was an excellent deal. It was just that corporate was over-leveraged. The banks just said no! The economy had taken a turn, and a few of the larger divisions were not doing well. The banks were nervous. I turned one hundred percent of my attention to the three divisions that were my responsibility. I was not going to spend more time on M&A until I was sure I had financing arranged beforehand.

The one customer I had been handling from the beginning requested my presence! I had developed such a good relationship with them that it was rare for me to have to visit. Everyone in my division knew the importance of this customer, so they were very well taken care of and always had my attention. The following day, I was on a plane!

The director of purchasing met me in the lobby. He informed me that I was to meet with the plant manager about a large project. The project involved the purchase of some of their equipment. We started toward the plant manager's office, but about halfway there, he met us and directed us to follow him into the plant. He explained that Corporate Headquarters sent a team into their facility to evaluate the effective use of floor space. Corporate Headquarters selected their facility to take on an extensive project which would ordinarily require a brick-and-mortar expansion. Corporate would prefer to outsource an under-utilized department in their facility to make room for the new project. The plant manager handed me a six-inch-thick binder containing a list of all the equipment they wanted to sell. The binder also included all the prints on the parts produced in that department. The plant managers requested an offer on the purchase of the equipment listed. Separately, individual quotations on the price to manufacture the parts. "Nice meeting you. When can you have that ready to present?"

I returned to my office and called in anyone I thought could help. We moved office furniture out of the way and spread everything out so we could see it all. It covered the floor, the walls, and every inch of the conference room, and we still had three inches of binder full of prints. We had to break it down into manageable sections. We worked for six straight days, ten to twelve hours a day. With the help of outside experts on pricing the used equipment market, we put a package together to present to corporate. Accounting prepared a pro forma cash flow analysis for the project from start to the first payment due. The cash required was going to be considerable. I thought this project had a chance because it would be very profitable, and I was hoping that that would be enough to get the banks to go along with it. I presented it to corporate, and they said NO!

I didn't want to give our very best customer the bad news over the phone, so I arranged to meet in person. The plant manager, purchasing manager, and accounting supervisor were all present. I explained the situation, and they were very understanding, but they concluded with, "You are the person that we want to handle this project."

I responded with, "What do you have in mind?"

"Go back to corporate and find out what terms would make this doable."

I called the VP of finance at corporate and passed on the request. The VP called me two days later and told me that corporate had no interest in the project. It was too small. They were working on a significant restructuring of financing with the banks, and they did not want to add this complication at this time. I asked to talk to the chairman of the board. The VP transferred my call to the chairman's office. I explained that I understood the situation, but I thought this was one of those once-in-a-lifetime opportunities, and I would like to take advantage of it personally. The response was, "I knew I was going to lose you eventually:

proceed, and if you can make it work, let's just arrange for a smooth transition. Good luck."

I approached my customer not with solutions but with problems. I informed them that corporate could not get involved under any agreement terms. I explained that I had started my own company five years ago with corporate's permission. I talked to the owner of the corporation about leaving the corporation and taking this project on personally. I received a green light. I want to take this on, but here are just some of the problems: finding enough space to rent, the cost of tearing down and re-rigging all the equipment, the cost to prepare proper foundations for the equipment, the terms for the purchase of expensive raw material (ten days), the negative cash flow, no bank will back this operation, and lastly the time it will take to staff this operation correctly. The division manager, also called plant manager, said, "This is good news, just give us a week, and we will see if we can make some of these problems disappear. In the meantime, you should start looking for adequate space." I was having a hard time believing that this was happening. Something was going on that I was not aware of, but I was not going to press the issue. There is a saying about "a gift horse in the mouth" or something like that.

Two weeks went by without a word, then sometime in that third week, I received a call from my customer requesting my presence for a meeting. I had to drive the six hours to get there because I did not feel it was appropriate to use the corporate aircraft for this trip. It did not take long to miss high-speed air travel. This project was my business, and to be present for a morning meeting, I had to make the drive the evening before the meeting and stay overnight in a hotel. The presentation went something like this: You will be responsible for finding proper

74

space to rent/lease, we will tear down and re-rig the equipment at our expense, and you will be responsible for the foundations, but we will provide you with the engineered designs, and prints of the foundations we installed at our facility. We will buy the raw material required and pay the suppliers in ten days; you will produce the product and ship at full price; we will invoice you for the raw material and give you thirty days to pay (this arrangement will expire in one year).

Staffing is your problem. Also, we have broken the entire project into three phases to help with cash flow. Finally, we propose a bailment agreement on the machinery and equipment, so you will not need to purchase the equipment, but we expect to gradually phase out that agreement starting the third year and ending by the fifth. "Now go see if you can make that work and review all this with your lawyer and accountant!"

I took the information and ran a cash flow analysis based on the proposal! The cash flow worked out to be positive. I went to a bank I had been dealing with and made my presentation for a line of credit. They were happy to approve the line I was asking for, but they required collateral for every asset I owned. My wife and I believed in maintaining a standard of living well below our income level.

On top of that, every year-end bonus, which had been substantial of late, went straight into our investment account. We both hated interest payments with a passion, so we never bought anything that we could not pay for well before the possibility of an interest charge. The only exception to that was our house. We both started working at minimum wage and lived at a minimum wage standard for some years which resulted in some good money management habits. We were very slow to increase our standard of living as compared to our income. The result was that we had a substantial net worth, and it was all going to be attached by the bank for the collateral the bank required to approve this deal. My wife and I sat together to address the question, "Do we want to do this?" Working for corporate, I was earning more than I ever had. Corporate was pleased with my performance, year-end bonuses were more significant than most people make in an entire year, and I had staffed my division with good people, so I was no longer working sixty and seventy-hour weeks. Did we want to give that up and risk everything we had for this opportunity? I was only forty years old and was receiving job offers frequently. We were confident that if for some reason this failed, we could do it over again, and if we were ever going to take the risk, now was the time. We signed with the bank, signed agreements with lawyers, found a building to lease with options on additional space for phases two and three, and I called corporate.

I gave the owner notice and promised I would not pirate any of his people. I would run ads for the people I needed and use the marketplace to fulfill my staffing requirements. His response was very complimentary. He said, "The one thing I am confident of is that you are an honorable person, and I trust you. However, I don't think you will be able to stop some people from moving over to your operation, and that is because of the way you manage." He then asked for my advice on my replacement and if I could recommend any current staff to take my place. I gave him two choices, which was the conversation's end.

I announced my departure and wished everyone well. The people working for my little painting company for the last five years had been busy preparing office space at my new facility and making arrangements for equipment arrival. They bought sawhorses, set them on the floor, laid old wooden doors across

76

the horses, covered the doors with table cloths, and those were our desks. There was no need for an intercom system because we were all going to be in the same office. I worked until the end of the workday on my last day. I then started to box up my personal belongings and say goodbye to the people that came to my office to wish me well. I left to go to my new office.

When I arrived, I saw people that came over from the division I had been running. At first, I thought they were helping, but they were setting up desks and moving in.

"What are you doing?" I asked.

"We are working for you," they replied.

"But we haven't had any discussions about money, or benefits, or anything. I promised corporate I would not steal any of the people from that division."

They replied, "You didn't steal us. We quit, and it's not only us, wait until you enter your new manufacturing facility!" I could not believe it. How could good people quit their jobs and come to work for me without negotiations regarding salary and benefits? I would call corporate in the morning!

I called and asked for the owner. I was transferred immediately and met with a chuckle on the other end, then, "I just won a bet! I bet that you would call. Some of your people gave notice when they got wind of your operation, but they wanted to surprise you, so we kept it from you. Don't worry. We will survive. Maybe one day you will be looking to buy one of our divisions. Just give me a call, and we'll talk!"

Chapter Eighteen

Rapid Growth

I was much better off than any other start-up company because so many key players came with me from a well-established, successful operation. Anyone who moved to my new company with me received the same salary, hourly rate, and benefits package they had at the other company. If I paid them fairly at the company I managed, I would do nothing differently now. We were all familiar with each other and the programs that had been established and refined those same programs applied at our new company. Still, we had to set up everything from accounting to purchasing, all while preparing for the arrival of the equipment designated as phase one. We set up timetables and deadlines that we coordinated with our customers. Every Monday, our customer sent an expeditor whose job was to prepare a progress report.

I was required to report in person every other week. It had been many years since I had to fly commercial. The convenience of private air travel spoiled me. I started taking flying lessons! I would rent a plane, fly to my customer with my flight instructor, and use the trips as training flights. I loved it! I was hooked! Most people have no idea about all that is involved in learning to fly. There are many tests a pilot in training has to pass to become licensed. You prepare for those tests by attending Ground School (classroom training) and actual flying under the supervision of an instructor. The areas of study are: weather, communications, the type of plane you will be flying, navigation, emergency procedures, and federal aviation rules and regulations. Flying can be safer than driving. I say it can be because, like everything else, piloting depends on good management. A pilot must manage the airplane maintenance, the logbook, the Jeppesen approach plates, the preflight procedures, and much more.

When a federal flight examiner approves you, you must stay current through refresher courses and documented flights. It has probably taken years and tens of thousands of dollars for most people to be knowledgeable and proficient enough to pass the final exam. All that can be lost, and your license revoked for any number of reasons, not unlike your driver's license. The federal government is the protector of the public by enforcing the agreement between itself and pilots to follow all federal aviation rules and regulations. Like any well-managed company, the federal government has a well-written policy and procedure book (FARS) that pilots and mechanics agree to abide by or lose their position. The people who fly and those affected by pilots flying depend upon the federal government enforcing those agreements. I was flying not just for business travel but as a hobby. I went on and received every rating except instructor.

I purchased my airplane and was able to avoid commercial travel. My customer appreciated that they could request my presence, and in a matter of a few hours, I would be at their door, especially at such a critical time. There were times when I would have to be at their office for a morning meeting, return home, land, and receive a message that I had to go back. These were hectic times. Eventually, we made it through all three phases, quadrupling our size, and because of the contractual arrangement, we ran a very positive cash flow. The bank gained confidence in the structure and even offered to extend our line of credit. The family's assets were no longer attached, and my wife was able to sleep at night! The company's growth was rapid; it was hard to catch up.

Everyone was working long hours and working hard. We started hiring people to lessen our workload but never altered our policy and procedure. Every new hire had to go through and pass the money management Class, the income statement class, the balance sheet class, and the return-on-investment class. All new hires had their first thirty days to read P&P, ask any questions about it, and then take the P&P test. If they passed the P&P test, they had to decide whether or not to sign a form agreeing to the terms and conditions of employment. I would sign that same form agreeing to enforce management's responsibilities. Many people did not make it past the hiring interview, and some did not make it past their first sixty days. The introductory classes served as an excellent screening process.

I was in my early forties, and when I would go through resumes and see dates, I would think I was looking at graduation dates, but what I saw were *birth* dates. How could this be? I had to face it, I was not getting any younger.

Chapter Nineteen

Dedicated Staff and Excellent Suppliers

My concerns shifted from running production and shipping quality parts on time to finding new business. It was apparent from the start that the reason for moving this particular department out was its limited life span. New designs and innovations have a way of rendering old techniques obsolete. What mattered was that the equipment I received was universal in its ability to produce a new product. I had to put my sales hat on and start a flow of new products before older models dwindled to nothing.

My relationship with this customer was highly advantageous, but I learned from working on acquisitions that a company with one customer is not a company at all. I had to work on building a much broader customer base and accomplish that before I had to start the purchase of all the equipment I received.

I was experiencing moderate success but was interrupted by an emergency request from customer number one!

My customer called and asked that I be present for an important meeting, and I should make hotel reservations in case the meeting carried over to the next day! I have to say I was worried, and of course, I feared the worst. When I arrived, Purchasing ushered me over to Engineering and into a conference room with no less than eight engineers present. A couple of them I had never seen before. The director of engineering started the meeting off, stating that for the first time, a new product they had engineered failed to pass testing by the Department of Transportation. They did not meet the requirements of the Federal Motor Vehicle Safety Standards Act, so we had to add something to this product that would solve every flaw discovered by the DOT.

For us to make the necessary corrections in the time frame allowed made this task exceedingly difficult. Having never failed these requirements, they were so confident about passing that they submitted their samples late. Typically, submission and approval are at least a one-year process. In nine months, all new production was going to begin, and if we did not have a solution, vehicles would come off the line and go into parking lots because they would not be safe to sell. A three-piece assembly was the answer. Two pieces had already been engineered and designed. The problem was the design of the third piece of that assembly. The director ended his presentation with, "The people in this room are responsible for coming up with the design of a solution. When we have that solution, we will turn it over to Purchasing to have that assembly produced by one of our suppliers. We all know it would not be possible to produce this in-house in a timely fashion, so we will have to find a supplier with a reputation of being able to operate without all the usual formalities." He was looking directly at me.

This problem was severe. I was hoping I could get out of it. I knew that anyone associated with this, should it fail, would be gone and forever forgotten as a supplier. I was sure I was not the only one in the room who understood that. We went straight to work, no stopping for lunch or dinner. The first thing we had to do was understand everything that was required of this assembly. The Federal Motor Vehicle Safety Standard Act (FMVSS) required many specifics, and we needed to understand the *why* of each one. The list was long, and some of the tests necessary were brutal. Then we went into brainstorming. Every idea ran into a wall somewhere down the list of requirements. Some good ideas failed when calculations proved that that idea would fail. After about twelve hours, our brains were numb. We decided to take a break and return to it in the morning. The next day was a repeat of the first, and about halfway through the third day, we called for a break. The suggestion was to take a day off and start back fresh. I put my pilot's hat on and blocked the assembly problem out of my mind. Flying is difficult enough when you are concentrating on nothing but flight. If you are preoccupied with something else, it's a dangerous endeavor. I flew home, ate a hearty meal, and went to bed.

The following day, I explained to my wife what was happening and how significant this problem was. It helped explain it to someone who kept asking questions to understand what made it so difficult. I had decided not to go into the office that day so that I could concentrate on the problem at hand. I decided to take a shower and clear my head! Sometime during that shower, an idea came to me. I did not know if this idea would work, or if it could be produced, but I had to run with it. I went to the kitchen table with a file folder, a six-inch scale, a pencil, scissors, and some tape. I made out of a piece of file folder the very first three-piece assembly. The idea was a good one. The proof needed to determine if this piece would pass the strength test remained. I called customer number one and told them I had an idea, but I would need some time to test it out and that it would be better if I stayed home rather than come to another meeting.

I went into the office and called in my tooling engineers, purchasing manager, and the head of the tooling department. I gave them a summary of what was going on and showed them my paper prototype. I told them that I had doubts about producing this thing out of metal, especially on a high-volume basis, so we needed to prove that it could be done before I went back to our customer.

The purchasing manager obtained samples of various raw materials, and the tooling engineers went to work drawing up details of a tool to perform the required tasks. The tooling department went to work making a prototype out of metal to replace my piece of the file folder. The purchasing manager also called in one of our best tooling sources, and that source sent in their top engineer. We accomplished this task because we had dedicated staff and excellent suppliers! I called the owner of a company where I had purchased equipment. His company also designed specialty high-volume assembly lines. None of my people went home before nine p.m. for the next three days. The only reason they went home at all was that I sent them home.

Based on all the input I received, I became confident enough to ask everyone involved in the project to start estimating the cost of all that would be required to make this assembly. I then made the call to my customer. My first contact was with the purchasing director and then the engineering director. I explained that I thought I had a solution and wanted to present it along with preliminary calculations. I was going to bring a paper mock-up and a few metal samples of details we used for testing.

The only thing they said was, when can you be here? I put everything in the plane and brought along one of my top engineers. We were in a conference room just before lunchtime. The following two hours were spent going over the design of the tooling: the testing, the calculations, the design of the assembly line, and the quality assurance concept. After the presentation, I received a vote of *no confidence*! At first, I could not believe it, then I was just sad and started packing up to go home. Before departure, the purchasing director explained that the problem was not the design but the ability to produce that design on a high-volume basis. The engineers were concerned that the quality requirements would have to be compromised, and the results would be catastrophic. I went home thinking that the program was dead as far as I was concerned.

That day, I reported to my group the failure to get approval and the reason. I explained that our customer liked the concept but felt it was one of those designs where you can make one, but you can't make millions and maintain quality. I went to my desk and looked at a week's worth of paperwork left unattended. I received a call from one of my suppliers. My purchasing manager had informed him of the results of my business trip. This particular supplier's business was the designing of assembly lines and conveyors. He asked that I visit their facility because he thought they had something that could help me with my assembly. I arrived the following day to meet with the owner and several people from his staff. They explained that ever since I involved them in this project, they had been working on something that would be a first for them, and they thought it was a solution to one hundred percent inspection and approval of every assembly produced. They knew of only one company in the United States that was using a similar system, and that was the Ford Motor Company. Ford was using it to one hundred percent inspect gears as the gears passed by on a conveyor.

A software engineer would write a program depicting the perfect assembly. Then create two other assemblies. Those two would represent the minimum and maximum allowable tolerances. The conveyor would stop at a station on the assembly line where three light sources and cameras would photograph the assembly. The photograph would go to a computer that would overlay the assembly and compare it to the three parts in its memory. If the assembly met all requirements, it would be allowed to pass on to packaging. If it did not meet all requirements, it would be stopped at the station before packaging and ejected from the line into a sealed container.

"Well, what do you think?"

I replied, "Please put some numbers together for me, and the time it would take to deliver this system."

I called the purchasing director and requested a meeting.

Chapter Twenty

"No Place on Earth to Hide."

When I arrived, all the top decision makers were waiting for me in a conference room. I told them I wanted to present them with an offer. First, I was confident I could produce the assembly per my last design. I could produce it at the volume required and to the specifications required. I could produce it and deliver it in the time frame required, but I must be released to begin within the next few days. Now, even if they should decide to release me, there is another problem. That problem is cash flow. The standard payment terms would make it impossible to purchase the necessary equipment and receive it in time, including progressive tooling necessary to produce the required stampings. If we can't overcome this obstacle, everything else is moot. From that point forward, the room was silent.

The director of purchasing asked me to wait in his office, and I did. He came in thirty minutes later and told me no engineer would put his or her name to the program. If I were to take this project on, I would be all on my own! If I succeeded, I would be their hero. If I failed, there would be no place on Earth I could hide!

I said, "What about the money?"

He said, "Any change to payment terms requires corporate approval, and that could take weeks, weeks we don't have."

I suggested progressive payments. I would break the project

into deliverables (things I could deliver and invoice for). That way, there would be a steady cash flow, and we could stay afloat! It was a risk, but we agreed on a handshake, and he gave me a verbal release with one last comment. He said, "My neck is on the block now too."

I returned home, and we immediately went to work! I will spare you all the details but that for the next seven months we worked hard and long. The most important thing to note here is that I never had to tell anyone who worked for me how many hours or days to work. I would go to work on Sunday, and people who needed to be there were there. Everyone did whatever they needed to meet or beat their timeline. Everything came together, we submitted samples on time, and the samples were approved. The first production run had a few wrinkles to iron out, but once again, everyone did what they needed to, and eventually, we were running at high volume. We never had to ship short of the quantity requested. We never ran negative on cash, and most importantly, we were making a profit. Our customer had given me a price target, and I was under that target, so everyone was happy, at least for now.

The product we were producing was on the market, and as it turns out, many of my customer's competitors were dealing with very similar issues. I started getting phone calls and requests for assistance. Within the next few years, we were producing assemblies of one type or another for almost every car company or supplier to a car company.

The company was doing very well, and I owe it to everyone who helped us get there. I had started a profit-sharing program that distributed proportionately seventeen percent of the profit into an Independent Retirement Account (IRA) for all employees.

Chapter Twenty-One

Life Happens

I made an appointment to see my doctor. I wanted him to look at what I thought was an ingrown hair on my neck. He looked at it and gave me an antibiotic to take for ten days and instructions to then return to him. He had measured the pimple-like structure on my first visit. On my next visit, he took another measurement and then advised me to see another doctor. Long story short, they thought it was Lymphoma. I must have cancer somewhere in my body, and the cancer has spread to the lymph system. So, the search began, appointment after appointment, test after test, none of which were pleasant. Finally, a meeting in which the doctors stated that based on other lumps appearing but no results from the tests, they were sure I had cancer, but they didn't know where it was. The cancer must be somewhere that they cannot detect. The only way they would know for sure would be to take a biopsy. The problem is that the biopsy could speed up the spread of cancer. I wanted to know for sure, so we scheduled a biopsy. They told me that while I was on the table, they could do a "frozen section" of a node and know right away and then remove any lymph nodes from that area.

It took three months to arrive at this point. I never said anything to anyone about what was going on. I have to say, I never felt in any way sick. Physically, I felt fine. Psychologically though, I knew I went through denial because I wasn't in denial any longer. The doctors took that away. So, I guess I was at the edge of anger, but the anger was coming out strangely. I was bound and determined not to have any further treatment or surgery. I did move into bargaining. I said to God, "Boy, if you can see your way clear to get me out of this, I will change. I know I have not been a good husband or father because I work long hours and days, but I will change that, I promise." I said that some number of different ways and some number of times.

I went in for the surgery, and the next thing I knew, I was coming out of the anesthesia but just barely. A nurse was on my right, and the doctor was on my left. I remember hearing the doctor saying, "Good news, it's not cancer!" I don't know if it was the anesthesia, but I could not grasp how I felt. Both feelings were running through my head at the same time. The doctors had put me through so much, so when I heard I did not have cancer, I was stuck between being angry and happy.

Before the surgery, I asked if someone could call my wife and tell her to come to the hospital by one p.m. and that I was having a minor procedure. While I was on my way to a room, the doctor called down to the waiting room and informed my wife that they had completed the biopsy and that the frozen section test of the lymph node was not cancerous. It was a parasite called Toxoplasmosis. My wife wasn't sure the doctor was talking to the right person, but after a short time, the communication got straightened out.

In most people, their immune system kicks in and resolves the parasite in a brief time. I have an immune deficiency that did not recognize this parasite, so it was multiplying in my blood system. The lymph system was trying to filter it out, causing the nodes to swell. The doctor kept me in the hospital overnight while administering sulfur-based antibiotics intravenously. I was happy to stay overnight because it gave my wife time to cool down. She was not at all happy about being kept in the dark!

I took a couple of days off from work to rest. I decided that from this point forward, I would go to work at eight-thirty and leave at five. I told my wife about the bargain I made with God. I promised to spend more time with her and the kids and never miss softball games, teachers' meetings, or anything else! God came through, so I will change and work an eight-hour workday and a five-day work week. No more working late into the night and no more weekends.

In less than three weeks, I called my wife from work at six p.m., letting her know that something had come up and I would be late. She said, "Okay, see you when you get home." Working late started all over again, gradually, but I knew where it was going, and it wasn't good! I hung up, sat at my desk, and asked myself, what's wrong with you? You make a promise to God, and he comes through, and you welch. You promised your wife you would leave work at five and sit here at six. What a disappointment you are. Is that who you are? Can't you keep a promise?

The following day, I made a phone call. The hospital had recommended a psychologist to talk to, to help me deal with the threat of cancer. I never contacted her but thought now would be a good time. I explained the whole story to her, and she just said that she did not work with people with my kind of *addiction*, but she offered a few recommendations. I said, "Thank you," hung up the phone, and said "*addiction*" about ten times. I was a "workaholic" and didn't know it! I thought I was a good provider and was becoming successful, which are admirable things in my mind. Being "addicted", being controlled by some addiction, being out of control, or not honoring my promise are all negatives! I need help!

Chapter Twenty-two

"One Really Great Lady!"

I did not enter into this therapy thing lightly. I asked many questions, read many books, and finally decided on a therapy that I believed would "fix me right up!" I figured six months later, I would be "all better!" I hope you are laughing because that is quite funny! I applied and was accepted to the therapy of my choice, which could have been the luckiest thing that ever happened to me!

I couldn't take six months off from work; I was worried about the company and all the people that worked for me if I did that (just a little indicator of my inflated ego!). I was able to work out a plan with my new therapist, who just happened to turn out to be one really great lady. I was on a new road, and at that time, I had no idea that it was a road with no end! I realized I would be absent more than ever before, so I had to prepare by hiring someone who could share my responsibilities. After this encounter with cancer, it became apparent that I was not going to live forever; I guess I thought I was, so it's just good staffing management to have someone capable and ready to step in. I looked around at the people that worked for me, they were all very good at what they did, but I did not see in any of them the right combination of talents to run this company. The next step was to put together a plan to minimize the risk of adding someone new at such a high management level.

I decided to rent a facility in the suburbs and move the engineering and design departments to that facility. Those two departments worked closely together and required very little direct supervision by me. Once they settled in, I moved the new tool construction and tool repair departments to that same facility. I went through the required efforts to incorporate that division as its own separate company. After a brief time, I announced that I was interested in hiring a person to head that division up. That person would be responsible for the profit and loss of the operation and communicate and coordinate all transactions between it and the manufacturing company. No one in the company expressed interest in the opportunity, so I began searching the marketplace.

One thing that made the search more difficult was the loss of my HR director. She had grown tired of the mid-west weather and decided to move to California. She was very good at sourcing and screening candidates. Her intuition was better than mine. I often considered an applicant qualified, and they probably were technically qualified, but she would pick up on some part of their personality that would cause a problem. I learned to defer to her because the few times I went forward against her recommendation, I lived to regret it!

I considered the need to replace the HR director more critical than any other hire at this time, so I devoted my efforts to that task primarily. I knew that I could not put off the hiring of the tooling division manager for very long, as both positions were critical for my transition to a lighter work week. After several interviews, I finally decided to make an offer to an HR candidate. She accepted and began the process of being introduced to our system.

I went over our entire management system during the

interview process. I explained the importance of maintaining the system's integrity, and most importantly, honoring all aspects of the agreement detailed in the company's policy and procedure. My evaluation of this applicant was that she was intelligent, had an agreeable personality, and seemed to get along well with everyone involved in the interview process. She thought the system was *genius* and loved the HR system. So did I, but I also know that people often tell you what you want to hear, and they call that salesmanship (which is just another way of saying deceptive). More than anything, I tried to emphasize that as HR director, her responsibility is *not* to advocate on the part of management *or* the employees. Her primary responsibility is to ensure both parties comply with the democratically agreed upon policy and procedure. Management should be making sure that employees are honoring the agreement, but sometimes it is management that is in violation. In those instances, she should first point that out to any individual manager, and if she is not satisfied with the resolution, then bring the matter to me. She is not a manager of the managers; she is the manager of P&P. On the other side of that coin, she has to monitor the employees and their adherence to P&P because sometimes, management fails to address issues that must be addressed. Again, bring any violation to the managers' attention first. If the issue is not resolved in accordance with the guidelines of P&P, then the matter must be brought to my attention. All of this is important because it is at the heart of fairness, and fairness is one of the main contributors to attitude and morale. Attitude and morale are critical to the success of the organization!

With the HR director in place, hiring a tooling division manager was less of a task for me. The HR director took care of the initial interviews. I only had to meet with those people that she considered possible candidates. Between the two of us, we narrowed it down to two choices. Once again, I hammered the importance of P&P and the entire system to the two remaining candidates. I emphasized the importance of their understanding that the people working for the company and their positive attitude toward the company is what makes the difference between failure and success. We, as managers, need to communicate with every person on an hour-by-hour, day-by-day basis. They can tell us what is going well and what isn't. Our job is to change whatever isn't going well so that their job is easier. The one candidate that seemed to grasp this better than the other is the one I hired. Fingers crossed, I hoped I was on my way to being able to back away from everyday duties and start to work on myself!

Chapter Twenty-three

Community!

By all measures, the company was doing very well. Our customers were happy, and the employees were in good spirits. Several customers awarded my company with "no-bid contracts" status, which meant that as long as my quotation for a new job was under what the customer estimated it should cost, I would be awarded the contract. As I walked through the plant visiting with each employee many times, I received suggestions for improvement that were very valuable. No one knows the job better than the person doing it. All I had to do was to get these suggestions implemented. People from the safety committee were attending seminars and coming back with ideas that improved safety and introduced new technology, resulting in hundreds of days without a lost time accident. Ideas that improved profitability and suggestions for safety were coming from the employees, which is a long way from strikes, walkouts, and shutdowns.

One day on a walk through the plant, I stopped to talk to one of the employees. I asked him how he was doing. He was not doing well because he was dealing with possibly having some teeth removed. He explained that a dentist could save his teeth, but our insurance did not cover dental, and he could not afford what the dentist would charge. I sent him to my dentist, and my dentist took care of his problem. I then started a self-funded dental and optical plan. Employee health and wellness was high on the priority list, not just the physical but also the psychological. I never liked the admonishment, "When you come to work, leave your problems at the door! Don't bring them in here! I don't want to hear about them." I never thought that was possible! State of mind can be a huge contributing factor to safety and accuracy. I know it was for me, so I connected with several different groups that ranged from counselors to psychologists to help people with the loss of a loved one, the pain of divorce, money problems, or any other issues.

We performed the random testing of employees for drugs and/or alcohol. The primary purpose is the safety of all others. If we determined that someone was having a problem with drug or alcohol abuse, we did not fire them if they went into a program for help. I would save their job, and they could return under a monitored program. If a leave of absence was necessary, they could return to work when their program administrator released them for work. They would then have to agree to an enhanced monitoring program. We just wanted to help eliminate the problem, not them.

Over time, certain developments took place quite naturally. Some young ladies working at the facility fell in love and got married. Then quite naturally, some would decide to start a family. One such young lady worked in the accounting department and was struggling to determine whether she would quit or try to continue working. Men don't have to decide that, and neither should women. I don't want to lose good people because they chose to have a family, so what to do?

I was struggling with my responsibility to this lady and her child. At first, I thought I would pay for daycare, but I read terrible news reports about abuse at what seemed to be reputable daycare organizations. I couldn't be part of anything like that. I did not know what to do and was explaining my dilemma to a friend one day; she said I should read a book by Jean Liedloff titled "The Continuum Concept."

After reading that book, I was left with two critical understandings. One was that nothing is more important to a child than its mother. Secondly, all those surrounding the mother have a responsibility to assist the mother in rearing that child. There is much more to it, but you must read the book. I had all I needed to know. I presented a new policy to the employees for approval and received it! I then took a second-floor office space with a bathroom, a kitchen, a private area for nursing, a play area, and a door with an electric lock. After giving birth and the approval of her doctor, a mother could bring her infant to work and move into that nursery area. A mother with an office job would have her desk moved to the nursery area along with any other files and communication equipment required. If she did not have an office job, we would restructure her job description so that her tasks would be administrative, and she could operate from the nursery. Nothing is more important than the child's care, so there was no requirement for absenteeism or attendance. It was the task of the community to assist the mother, should it be requested.

Accounting would convert the mother's salary into an hourly rate. She was responsible for keeping track of the hours worked versus the hours spent caring for the baby. The mothers were compensated for the hours spent caring for the baby and the hours worked. One-half of the baby care hours were a loan. That loan would accumulate over the time she remained in the nursery program. Should she leave the employ of the company, we would agree on a payout plan. The company would forgive a fixed percentage of the loan every full year the mother remained employed with the company. The objective of this policy was that no woman that decided to start or add to her family would have to decide to quit her job. No woman would have to suffer the loss of income because she chose to have a child. No woman who worked for me would feel she was on her own with difficulty caring for her child. No woman would have to turn her child over to anyone else for care.

The lady working in the accounting department that started me thinking about this has worked for me since graduating from college. She was the first to become pregnant and enter the nursery. She had *triplets*! Others followed, but she was the first, and I am quite proud of having developed this program. At that time, I knew of no other company having a program remotely similar! Some twenty-five years later, she is still working for me, and so are two of her now five sons.

I tell this story as a way to communicate an overall management philosophy. The company has to earn enough of a return on investment to remain in business. True for the owner as it is also true for anyone. We have to work together for the health of the company. If the company's earnings exceed the target ROI, a portion of that excess gets proportionately shared with everyone qualified for profit sharing. The company's existence has to be for the benefit of the people that care for it. A company with a method of payment that assures each employee is compensated fairly and a benefits package that exceeds industry standards gave me every reason to believe that my reduced daily involvement would not be a problem. But then one day several managers asked to speak to me in private!

Chapter Twenty-four

Strength of Conviction

Three managers who had worked for me before I started this company were complaining about the HR director. It boiled down to her becoming an advocate of the people rather than the P&P. They had specific details on violations of P&P by their staff members. When taken to task, the HR director argued on the employee's side against the managers, which is fine if the managers violate the P&P agreement. The managers referred to her as a "bleeding heart" because she would feel sorry for the employees and want to overlook offenses. The managers knew that if HR allowed some people not to be held to the requirements of P&P, the result would be attitude and morale going off the cliff's edge. I asked them to leave me with the examples that they brought to me. I would investigate and get back to them.

I asked my assistant to pull the personnel files involved, and I pulled out my copy of P&P. After a thorough review, I asked to see the HR director. I will not go into the details of the instances brought to my attention. Suffice it to say that we were dealing with clear violations of P&P, and there was every reason for the employees to have the violations brought to their attention and recorded for loss of points at their following review. The HR director had fallen into the trap of wanting to let people get away with a violation of P&P, thinking that then she would be liked. She tried to use the "as long as rules are absolute…" statement in

P&P as a logical argument against taking people to task for violations. Management must consider each circumstance, so we went through each case one by one. I asked the HR director to explain what circumstance would mitigate the violation of P&P. One terrible answer was thinking that if we lessened the consequences, the offender would be happy and have a good attitude, which would be good for morale. I directed her to its impact on all the other people and their attitudes. When people see that management is selectively applying the rules in P&P, they will think that P&P does not matter. That smacks of favoritism, and that is a violation of fairness. Her response was silence. So, I decided to have her meet with each manager and the employee involved. It was her responsibility to explain to the employee the justification for the manager's action. I would consider this a teachable moment and hope she would better understand her responsibilities.

She offered her resignation after completing the meetings she was required to attend. So, I was back to looking for a new HR director. I went through three more before I found one that could stand up for P&P and understand the importance of that. An HR director has to care more about being respected for the strength it takes to call out either side.

I decided to draft a new policy for presentation. It was called the "Appeals Process." I would teach a "Management Training" class. Graduates from the class would be eligible to sit on a management review panel. The process went like this: if an employee disagrees with an action on the part of a manager, they can appeal that action to the HR director, if unhappy after that appeal, an employee or manager can appeal directly to the CEO, if still not happy a person could appeal to the management review board, and the board's decision (on a majority rules basis) is final. At any stage of the appeal, the action taken could be overruled, instated, reduced, or enhanced. This policy was voted on and approved. I believe that any new HR director would appreciate the new policy. I know I did because it turned out to be very effective in the following months and years.

Back to the marketplace searching for a new HR person. It took several more attempts and a lot longer than I had hoped, but finally, I had a person capable of performing the HR task. I believed I had the right people in place and was anxious to make the final move. The person responsible for engineering and tooling had been interacting successfully with the people in the manufacturing division. He had established himself as knowledgeable and personable. He managed to grow that division and meet ROI targets. I decided to bring the engineering and design departments back in-house. Shortly after that, the tooling department followed. I offered the director of that division the plant manager's position, and he accepted. From this point forward, I removed myself from day-to-day activities. I decided that one of my primary responsibilities would be Corporate Pilot, which didn't last long. As much as I love flying, I hated sitting around in the pilot's lounge waiting for salespeople to appear for the return trip home. When appropriate, I would hire a pilot qualified to captain my plane to transport company people to whatever event they needed to attend.

Chapter Twenty-five

"Stay the Course!"

The company was doing well. After people settled into their new positions, my wife and I started to schedule vacations. My wife does not like to fly because she experiences an issue with motion sickness. We managed to get by with the help of some medication, but it wasn't any fun for her. We would arrive wherever we were going, and she would spend the first day sleeping off the meds. Over the next two years, we vacationed in Florida, Texas, Massachusetts, West Virginia, and California. We decided we would concentrate on California. We spent the next couple of years picking spots along the coast. We would spend a couple of weeks in different cities at different seasons of the year. We decided California was the state we wanted to retire to, but we didn't know what city in California.

One day we were flying to visit one of our children at the university she was attending. My wife and son were in the cabin. I was flying, but I hired a first officer for this trip. I had been properly trained by many private instructors and Flight Safety International. Everything was going along just fine as we leveled off at thirty-two-thousand feet. Shortly after that, we heard a muffled pop. A red cabin pressure warning light came on within the next thirty seconds. When the cabin pressure warning light comes on, you put on your oxygen mask, drop the masks for the cabin, pull the throttles back to idle, and begin an emergency descent. You put the nose down while simultaneously banking the plane into a forty-five degree angle turn. The object is to get the aircraft down to at least ten thousand feet as fast as you can safely! While the pilot in command is doing this, the first officer is communicating to Air Traffic Control that we have an emergency and are conducting an emergency descent.

We were lucky that we did not experience a rapid decompression. Instead, a hose that connects a pump to the cabin somehow separated from the cabin connection. That pump pushes air into the cabin to keep it pressurized. Once that happened, we were gradually subjected to a loss of pressure, thus the warning light. We returned home and turned the plane over to the mechanics. My wife decided she would only fly commercial, if at all. It was hard for me to give up the plane, but it made no sense to keep it if we were not going to use it. We sold the plane!

I had to think about what I would do with my time. I did not want to go back to work full time. I was enjoying being so much less involved with the company. I wasn't taking a salary, just quarterly disbursements of profit. We were financially well off, so we were reaping the rewards of many years of hard work. Our son had been going to work with me ever since he was ten years old. He had gravitated to engineering and was tutored by some of the best in the industry. I decided to promote the plant manager to CEO and my son to VP. The two of them would meet with me once a month to review financial reports. I had handed them a management system that, over the many years, had resulted in a performance at the top one percent of other companies in our business.

I was confident that, if they stayed the course, the company, and all the people in it, would be safe and secure. I did make a few benefit changes before the final turnover. When I started the company, I did not create a pension plan because most pension plans had a ten-year vesting requirement. If an employee left the company in less than ten years, they received nothing. I had decided to do an annual profit-sharing disbursement the year after I received audited financials. The problem with that is that people were almost immediately spending the money. Some number of employees reached the point where they had children getting ready to go to college, but they had not saved for that occasion. I changed the profit sharing to an IRA program with immediate vesting. Secondly, I started a college loan program at the lowest interest rate the IRS would allow. An employee would be able to co-sign for their child and borrow a percentage of their annual salary every year. To qualify for a loan, the student had to declare a major. That major had to have a marketplace value that indicated the likelihood of being able to pay back the amount borrowed. These additions were my final additions to benefits for the employees. I turned the company over to my son and the newly appointed CEO.

Chapter Twenty-six

"Obligation!"

We took a vacation to meet with some friends in Santa Barbara. Our friends suggested we join them on a trail ride in the hills. For as long as I can remember, I loved horses but never had the time to learn how to ride. I jumped at the opportunity to ride one. Maybe it was all those cowboy programs I grew up with: Hop-a-long Cassidy and his horse Hoppy, Roy Rogers and Trigger, Zorro and Diablo. I could name more, but you get the point. Once, when I was ten, I asked my dad to take me to the park to ride a horse. When we got there, my father saw how much it cost, which was the end of renting a horse. So, horses were out of the question until now! I was looking for something my wife and I could do together, and I thought this was it! At one point on the trail ride, we cantered up a hill. The trial guide was in front of me, and his seat appeared glued to the saddle. I was bouncing, slipping, sliding, and was surprised I stayed on. When we got to the top of the hill, I asked the guide how he managed to do that. He said, "Heck, I don't know. I've been riding ever since I was a kid, but I understand there are people that teach riding." When we returned home, we did a little research and found a riding stable that offered to give riding lessons, and we made an appointment.

We then started renting horses to take lessons, bought our horses, and built our horse farm. When we first started, we knew nothing, but it did not take long to learn that it takes a lifetime to become good at horsemanship. What we did know was that we loved horses, and we wanted to take care of them properly. The first trainers that we hired to teach us were people that were much more interested in money than they were in the horses. They loved meeting people like us because they could make much more money selling us horses than they could giving us riding lessons. We trusted them, and they took advantage of that trust. We set out to learn enough to protect ourselves and searched for people that had established reputations for being trustworthy.

Once we became somewhat proficient at riding, we tried the sport of jumping horses. It didn't take long to find out that most people do not spend the time to learn how to train a horse to jump. Horse and rider will be damaged if not trained to jump correctly. We wanted no part of that. Unfortunately, it seems that when making money with horses is the priority, the horse suffers. Finally, we met a man schooled in the classical art of dressage. We met him while he was giving a riding clinic. I bought books he had written and read passages like, "The horse was not designed to carry weight above his back. If you take him out of nature to use him for transportation without proper conditioning, you will shorten his useful life. You have to learn to condition him in order to enhance and extend his life beyond what nature would provide." That conditioning is called "dressage". I immediately went to work trying to convince this man to come to our farm to give clinics. I wanted him to teach us riding, dressage, and horsemanship. I sought his advice on how to manage everything from feeding to breeding. He agreed, and his training led my wife, me, and all the trainers that worked at our farm to become one of the premier stables in the area.

Until this point, we had purchased horses that had been

"broke" to riding, and we knew next to nothing about how to start a young "never-been-ridden" horse. Some of the horses we purchased were started inappropriately and developed behavioral problems. I had heard about trainers whose specialty was starting and correcting horses that had problems or were dangerous. I signed up for a few clinics with one trainer out in Colorado. This particular trainer ran an apprenticeship program. I signed up, and my wife and I spent the next seventeen months traveling back and forth to Colorado from the mid-west to apprentice with this man. The more I learned, the more I appreciated this gift of nature we call a horse.

The horse, the airplane, and the company are similar in many ways. First, there is much to learn to *properly* manage any of the three. Second, when you take ownership, you become responsible for the care and well-being of everyone involved. Suppose you are selfish in using or abusing any of the three solely for your benefit. In that case, you diminish their potential and possibly cause serious harm. After ten years of proper training, my wife and I became discouraged because so many horse owners were not interested in doing right by the horse. The horse was there for their glorification and fun. They were not willing to work at learning how to properly dressage the horse. In my opinion, if you decide to take on people or things, you are obligated to understand their wants and needs. You are further obligated to provide for them accordingly. If you accomplish this, I believe you will enjoy success.

Unfortunately, many boarders at our farm were unwilling to invest the time and effort required to dressage their horse. I suppose it was naïve of me to think that if you love horses and have been educated about that which is best for the horse, what would naturally follow is that is what a person would do. In the horse world, there is no outside force that requires horse owners to classically dressage their horse. Only life-threatening abuse of the horse can initiate action by several agencies. My wife and I decided that we would prefer to practice privately. The next time someone offered to buy our farm, we accepted the offer. We decided it was time to move to California! We found a place to board our horses in Woodside, California, and bought a condo in San Francisco.

Over the next ten years, I traveled all over Eastern Europe, training with world-class horsemen (and women). I purchased a few horses in Denmark, the Netherlands, and a few in Germany. Three of them were stallions, and all were just three years old. I had them shipped to Woodside, where I rode every day to train these horses under the occasional instruction of clinicians brought to the farm from all over the world.

I would receive quarterly financial reports from my son and the CEO of the company. The performance had been falling off and was at an all-time low. The company was still making money but just barely. During the last ten years, I worked with lawyers to prepare something called an "Intentionally Defective Grantor Trust." It is just a trust set up to transfer company shares to our children. My wife and I were financially secure. None of our assets were attached to secure loans for the company. The year was 2008. My son called! He was in a panic, the market crashed, and the automotive world was in crisis. "Dad, I need your help!"

Chapter Twenty-Seven

Back in the Saddle

If the manager of a private business makes significant errors, that private business suffers. If the federal government mismanages, the entire country suffers! The housing industry was collapsing. The government had been guaranteeing home loans that private banks would not ordinarily make. The banks would make the loans and sell them to the government at a profit. The banks took advantage of a flawed federal government program. It spiraled up until it came crashing down. It was like building a skyscraper on quicksand, and the crash caused panic. The bank we had been dealing with for twenty-five years was in trouble. Another bank came in and purchased our bank and issued an edict to all customers that primarily supplied the automotive industry. That edict went something like, find another bank and fast! That bank was under the assumption that the automotive companies would go belly up, and they wanted no part of dealing with the bankruptcies that would follow.

We were in a good position because we had significant cash and a stellar record. All banks were in the same difficult situation: they wanted any line of credit secured with liquid assets. Thus, my son called my wife and me asking for help! I flew home for an emergency meeting with my son and the company CEO. They gave me all the necessary financial information and pro forma future forecasts. I had to decide if I would put our assets up for collateral with the bank. My final decision was that the federal government would not let the three largest automotive companies go out of business. There were thousands upon thousands of middle-class workers in the auto industry. I believed politicians would not let all those people lose their union jobs, not because they cared about the people but about what would happen in the next election. I was not too fond of having some significant part of our assets attached by a bank. We had been free and clear of any such loans for so many years that it was disappointing. A considerable negative was that everything was happing so fast. The bank left us no choice. We had to decide in a short time. I made it clear to my son and the CEO that if my assets were at risk, I would again be involved in the company on a day-to-day basis. We agreed they had no other choice, and one week later, the new bank sent the loan agreement papers to us in San Francisco. My wife and I signed, and we made arrangements to rent a place back home for what we hoped was just six months or so.

I planned to commute from San Francisco, work at the company for a week, offer some direction, and then return to San Fran. After my first visit to the manufacturing facility, I knew that plan would not work. I had held onto the image of the company and how it looked before I left. What I saw was something different. To start with the place was dirty, the equipment was dirty, the floors were dirty, even the people looked like they were wearing the same clothes every day. The first thing I did was to let my son know that I was disappointed in his performance.

I then went looking for the CEO. It was then that I found out that he had been working remotely from home, as were my son and the accounting department manager. I would have to deal with it sometime later. Right now, this place needs to get clean. I called the maintenance department supervisor and asked for cleaning supplies. The inventory of cleaning supplies was non-existent. I called the purchasing department manager and asked why. He told me that he had been instructed not to purchase anything that was not part of a final assembly, and this had been going on for quite a long time. I told my son to go home! I knew he was having trouble with his wife and that he should take care of that before I saw him back at the plant. I shut the plant down and called for a brief meeting to announce that I was taking over. When I did that, I saw very few faces from the past. There were many new people that I had never seen before. As the new management made changes, people gradually left, and those who left were some of the best.

I went to see the HR director. I went there to see any changes made to the original P&P Manual. He smiled and said that the P&P manual had been retired! My head was spinning after hearing that remark. I told him I needed to add to the staff because I needed to get the company cleaned up, starting with the floor. I told him that I slipped on oil on the way to his office and almost fell. That is a major safety violation. He said, "Well, adding to staff is a problem because here in the inner city, we can't get anything but the scum of the earth." I told him not to worry about getting me any people because, as of right now, you don't work here any more. Please leave. That was the beginning of an improvement in attitude and morale. Next, I called the CEO and accounting supervisor and told them that working from home was over for them. I expected to see them in an office at the plant at eight a.m. every day and that the workday ended at five p.m.

The next stop was the purchasing manager's office. He worked for me from the very beginning of the company. I told him I needed oil dry (a sawdust-like material used to absorb oil spills) and lots of it. I wanted operators to spread it all over the floor, sweep it up and properly dispose of it. I told him that this project was his to manage and was a high priority. He told me that the CEO stopped purchasing oil dry when he cut everyone's pay because of the loss of business they experienced a while back. Cutting everyone's compensation is a terrible decision. The people working in the plant should not have to pay for management's mistakes.

Next, stop the accounting department. I asked to see payroll records. After a review, it was apparent that management decided to reduce everyone's pay *except* for the major managers in the company! I could not believe what I had discovered. It wasn't even lunchtime. "Shut the plant down. I want another meeting." At that meeting, I announced that I was returning everyone's pay to what it was before any reduction. I will return to you the money you have lost. Accounting will need a few days to figure that out, but you will receive that as back pay in a separate check. My rule has always been that when we have to cut back, we do that at the top, not from the people that can afford it the least. I will be working for no salary as CEO of the company.

The next day I met with the (ex) CEO and the accounting department manager. I told them that I fired the HR person and that I needed someone to at least take care of the task of making sure all personnel documents were in order. The accounting manager smiled, and I asked her why. She said, "That's all he was doing anyhow. Who is going to do HR?" I said that I would take care of that for now. I suggested that she contact one of the local universities and ask to hire an intern to take care of the personnel files. Her response was another smile. I also told her that the old CEO would become our sales manager and his salary would be immediately reduced to that of the sales manager. I then asked the old CEO if he was okay with that, and he said, "Yes."

Over the following weeks and months, I discovered that the production supervisor was the brother of the old CEO and that he knew very little about what we do. I assigned him particular projects and asked him for deadlines of his own making. One day when meeting with him and asking for progress reports on his responsibilities, he appeared angry. I asked him what was bothering him, and he said he did not like working "this way." I asked him, "What way is that!" He did not like my checking up on his progress. He said he is not used to that, he is used to just being given a task, and when it is done, he is done, and that is that. I explained to him that what I do is called management and that if he is going to work for me, that is how it will be. Later that day, he told me he couldn't work that way because it caused him anxiety and upset his stomach. I said, "Sorry, I guess you will have to leave." The next words out of his mouth were quite unbelievable. First, he said I could not fire him because no one else could do his job, and then he said that his brother hired him so that I couldn't fire him. I called his brother, and his brother fired him.

One other thing that was obvious to me was that the scheduling system I had established was missing. I asked supervisors on the floor how they knew what job to run and in what order. They said that all scheduling was on the computer in the office now, and they had to deal with the production scheduler. I am all for upgrades due to technology, but I had to investigate this further. The production scheduler walked me through the system, and during my education session, I learned two things: one was that the system was twenty-four to forty-eight hours behind real-time, and the other one was that the production scheduler was a good friend of my son's. When I investigated further, it was evident his pay was not in line with marketplace research. Favoritism kills attitude and morale. I offered him a new justifiable salary. I put him in charge of reinstituting the old system so that we would be making decisions based on real-time needs. He accepted the responsibility and the new salary with a "Yes, sir." I think previous actions were starting to take effect.

A lady who worked for me for several years before I retired called me. She wanted to meet to say hello. We met after work, and she said she heard that I was back. She wanted me to know that she was not happy working for her current employer. I offered her a job as my HR director. She accepted! We spent the following weeks putting together a new P&P manual and submitted it to a local lawyer specializing in labor relations. It was approved and submitted to the employees for approval! It was well received.

We were well on the way to recovery, but there was so much more to do. The sales manager was doing an excellent job of bringing in new opportunities. In the past, engineering would provide him with basic information so that he would have a general idea of the price, but from there, he was in the dark. He thought the best he could do would be to negotiate with the customer. I was doing the estimating now and at the same time setting up the standard cost system, which was another abandoned system.

My son and the CEO abandoned many tried and true systems, and I didn't know why. I thought at first that it was laziness because the systems did require effort to maintain. Then I thought, maybe the CEO thought his changes were more efficient or better, and lastly, that the old systems were just plain unnecessary. One thing I knew for sure was that the changes resulted in a financial decline.

The big surprise to me was that he took over a group of people and a system of management that was yielding results in the top one percent of all companies in the same business. All he had to do was keep it going! He decided to abandon existing systems and hire unqualified friends and relatives. He was using the company for his benefit and at the expense of all the other people working there. I had been involved with other companies that were able to continue to survive despite such poor management, but it never ceased to amaze me.

I was making changes, but they were changes that were bringing us back to the system that had been working. Every month the financials indicated that they were the right changes. Attitude and morale were also improving. Most importantly, the one-hundred and sixty people working there greeted me with a smile and bid me "Good morning" every day.

One of the changes had to do with pricing a new potential product. I would give the sales manager the price we were to ask for, but I would give him some percentage within which he could negotiate. I told him that if he always needed to use the full share of allowable price reduction afforded, it would reflect negatively on him. Years ago, while running a company for corporate, I developed a pricing system that resulted in a high percentage of requests for quotations becoming purchase orders. There is no reason why we should not be able to do that again without giving away the store.

Another change I had to make was with my son. It was time to address my son and his future involvement with the company. I explained that I came back at his request and would never do it again. He knows how I manage and all the systems that worked so well. He knows it's about the people that work at the company, and the company exists for the benefit of the people. *Not* the other way around. Every principal has been violated under your supervision! I expect that when I leave, it will happen again. I suggest we hire a new CEO who can fully embrace the programs and methods we employ because it is obvious that the old CEO could not. It was hard for my son to hear me say these things, but they needed to be said. As an explanation for his behavior, he confessed that he had removed himself from the company for several years. His marriage was in trouble, and he was trying to save it. I told him I understood how difficult it must have been for him and that I would stay on until we found the right person to take over. In the future, he will not be responsible for the entire company's performance. I would like for him to take over the engineering department.

I was going to work every day just like in the old days, walking the floor and making changes to operations. So many times, the changes seemed minor, but they add up to improvements in productivity, attitude, and morale. Just making observations, like one part of the plant being cold in the winter and adding heaters or hot in the summer and adding fans to improve working conditions. Things like buying soft rubber pads for people to stand on to make it easier on their legs. Looking for improvement to operations by asking people about the tasks they perform and any difficulties they may have. I started teaching classes again on money management, budget, income statements, balance sheet, and interest expenses.

I reinstated the wage and salary review committee and the standard cost accounting system. It took four years to get the company back on its feet. The facility was clean. The equipment and the floors were freshly painted, the safety committee reinstituted, and a safety director installed. The old scheduling system was up and running, and so was the trimester employee review system. The company was back on top. The company supported people who wanted to get ahead by paying for their education.

We were teaching classes in-house for specific jobs so people could move up in position, and we used the marketplace surveys to ensure that everyone would be paid fairly. Attitude and morale were high, and people were happy, as evidenced by how many wanted friends and relatives to come to work there. Our best new hires were people that were recommended by current employees. It turned out that the person making the recommendation acted like an additional supervisor of the person newly hired. They would say, "Now, don't you embarrass me! This job is a good opportunity." Employees were enthusiastic. They would make suggestions for improvement to their supervisors and feel good about their contribution when they see their suggestions implemented. We were making money just like in the old days. Profit contributions were once again being deposited to employee IRA accounts. Most importantly, my wife and I were free and clear of any encumbrances.

Now, I just needed to find the right CEO.

Chapter Twenty-eight

The People's Policy

I wouldn't be able to return to retirement until I found the right person to take over. I would want to spend at least six months with the new CEO to be sure whomever it was would be on track before I left. I contacted our bankers, our accounting firm, an Equal Employment Opportunity Firm we had worked with, and the president of an association we had belonged to for over twenty years. After about six weeks, I had three appointments to meet with my first three candidates. All three looked good on paper, but I wanted to meet each one in an informal setting and start with first impressions. If I have a positive first impression, the interview process begins. We would meet again and begin to share information. One candidate submitted a request for financial reports for the last five years. His list of requests was long and required several days for me to put together. I required that he sign a non-disclosure agreement. After it was signed, I provided the information requested. We met again one week later. We both had a list of questions as we interviewed each other. One question surprised me. This particular candidate had noticed that our rate of absenteeism and tardiness was exceptionally low. He reviewed that policy in P&P and wondered how I managed to obtain approval from the majority on such a strict policy. I explained that I did not dictate the procedure and that there was a long story about how it came into being. He said he would like to hear it, so I started with, "Many years ago, there was a man that worked for me at another company. He was our 'Don Quixote', so let's call him Don." I explained that Don was very good at what he did for us, but he seemed to get into trouble after hours. His misadventures often resulted in him arriving at work late or not at all. When he did arrive, everyone wanted to hear about his latest adventure. A bar room brawl or the time he came in with a black eye and his wife made him sleep on the front porch for coming home at three in the morning. Don liked to drink on Friday after work, severely affecting his judgment. You could say that many of his fellow employees lived vicariously through Don. He was well-liked for his entertainment value, and when he came to work, he was better than most at his job. Addressing Don's attendance posed a dilemma. He had been issued the proper warnings according to the old P&P but to no avail. The next step would be termination. Many employees felt Don's absenteeism was justifiable because he had legitimate reasons for missing work. If I fired Don, their perception would be that I was being unfair. If I did not follow the P&P, then I was saying that P&P was arbitrary. If that was true, then fairness was just a word, not a practice. I decided to call a company meeting. I asked Don if I could use him as an example in this meeting and hopefully save him from termination. He gave me his permission. I presented the employees with my dilemma. Then I asked for a vote on whether or not we should have a policy on absenteeism and tardiness. "Why not just come to work and get paid for your time here? You come and go as you please. Let's take a vote!" There was a pause, and several people asked to take the floor. Long story short, it was evident that in a manufacturing environment, many people depended on others to do their job efficiently. It would be a significant inconvenience to many others if someone were not dependable. The great majority decided we needed to enforce an attendance policy. So, what should that policy be? We opened the floor for suggestions! One person who had not been late or missed a scheduled workday in ten years thought there was no reason for being late or absent and suggested that either should result in termination. The majority thought that was too harsh and offered examples of situations that any reasonable person should consider. Around and around we went, and we finally came up with the existing P&P regarding absenteeism and tardiness. The policy they came up with had more severe repercussions than anything I would have tried to introduce. I asked if anyone wanted to be in charge of enforcing this policy, and I had no takers, so I said I would take on the responsibility of enforcing *their* policy. We also voted on giving Don a clean slate to start over on, and he became a very reliable employee and still had many stories to share!

From that date forward, I was not enforcing my policy or the company policy, I was enforcing *their policy*. Anyone with a complaint could take it up with the great majority of their fellow employees.

The candidate expressed some wonderment still at the fact that the employees volunteered such a strict policy. He thought they would have leaned toward a much more liberal set of rules when presented with an opportunity to develop an approach on their own. My answer was that I would agree with him if it were any of many other companies. We educate our people on matters that directly affect their job security. They understand that we must be competitive within the marketplace.

An example would be the understanding of ROI and that it's not that we are making money, it's are we making enough money to continue with the investment in this company. The people here are not afraid of hard work. They are very interested in being treated fairly, having job security, and the opportunity to get ahead. If they should vote on something that makes us less competitive, they are one step closer to putting us out of business.

The list of questions was long on both sides, much too long to go over in detail here. Several meetings were required, but as they progressed, both parties were moving toward an agreement! I called my son and let him know the current status of the interview process. I told him that I had at least two candidates that looked very promising and that I thought I would be deciding within the next few months. He offered me an update that was a bit of a surprise. He had been divorced for about six months and told me he had met the love of his life. The only surprise was that I usually knew who it was he had fallen in love with. My son had fallen in love every six months since he was sixteen.

Chapter Twenty-nine

My Way is Not the Only Way

A long time ago, I decided to invest in real estate. I formed a real estate investment company to handle those transactions. Lawyers and accounting firms advised that for estate planning purposes, I should designate our two children as the owners of the investment firm. It's not necessary to go into all the details about how it gets arranged, but as the years advanced, I paid off one large building I had decided to purchase. The investment firm owned the building free and clear.

The doorbell rang, and I answered the door. It was my son. He presented me with a giant check and some papers to sign. I asked what this was all about, and he explained that the payment was for the balance due on the Intentionally Defective Grantor Trust. Ordinarily, it would take years to pay down the final amount, so I was surprised and asked him about the source of the money. The two children agreed to borrow against the building they now owned, so they could pay off the trust and take ownership of the company. My son explained that now with the divorce over and he had found his one true love, he would be able to concentrate on running the company himself, so I need not pursue hiring a CEO. I told him that he was in control of the company. I had very little to say about it, but my advice would be to add the right CEO to keep the company going on the current path. His response was, "Dad, your way is not the only way." I said, "Of that, I am sure I wish you the best of luck."

That meeting was tough for me. It was apparent that my son was not happy with my loss of faith in his ability to run the company, and he wanted to prove that he could. I was concerned that one hundred and sixty families would be affected if he once again failed to perform. I made it clear that he could never return to his mother and father for financial aid. If he failed, he failed, and the wealth we provided him with would be at risk. He said, "Maybe that is why I will not fail this time." I hoped it was true! I later discovered that he decided to bring back some of the same people I had either demoted or dismissed, and he was bringing back the old CEO as CEO. I was sad! But we would live out the rest of our lives without ever again putting our finances at risk.

Chapter Thirty

My Way?

When my son said to me, "Your way is not the only way," I knew it was a true statement. I started thinking about how and why my way came to be. I came up with two significant factors. One factor is that I was compelled to correct interactions between management and employees that I believed to be wrong. My work experience exposed me to negative interactions between management and employees. These negative interactions were morale killers! A positive attitude and enthusiasm amongst the workforce can make what seems impossible happen. A negative attitude and morale can cause a company to feel like it is going forward with the brakes applied.

In some ways, unions resolve some wrongs but also cause other wrongs. Unions are a company in their own right. They have employees and overhead that they have to pay. They have expenses, and they expect to earn a profit. They need to charge companies to cover those expenses. These charges may cause a company to be less competitive than other companies in the same business and threaten job security to the people in the company they represent. Unions negotiate wages and benefits on behalf of the employees, and powerful unions can become so aggressive in their negotiations that they cause a company to go bankrupt. It was obvious to me that many managers committed grave errors, and the people should be protected. That is a service a union can provide. It was also evident that unionized companies have their fair share of shortcomings. I thought if only management set up systems to take care of the needs of people, there would be no need for the additional burden of the union. I wanted the best of both worlds! I had to right the wrongs.

A critical issue is fair compensation. I believe it is wrong for one group in a company to have a different benefit package than all the others.

I believe the fairest method to determine compensation is shopping in the marketplace for highly qualified people. I developed the Wage and Salary Survey Committee to research the market on the cost of each job description.

I believe a company must provide a safe, clean, environmentally friendly facility.

I believe employees want to know where they stand with supervision. In what ways are they performing well, where do they need improvement to increase their compensation, and how can the company help them? I developed a trimester review system to help people earn more, ask them about their goals and objectives, and support them in reaching their goals.

I believe it is essential for management to share financial performance because it affects the security of every person in the company. To prepare people for the presentation of financials, I started teaching classes on the tools presented by accounting and then shared financial performance quarterly.

I believe management reaping all the rewards of a company's performance is wrong, so I put a proportionate profit-sharing plan in place.

I believe it is wrong for management to dictate rules to the workforce with a take it or leave it attitude, so I negotiated P&P with the people democratically.

The primary directive is "As long as rules are absolute, there can be no justice." I believe it is wrong to follow the rules blindly because circumstances are infinite, so I put in place a grievance procedure to empower employees and reduce the fear of losing employment over a minor infraction. I put in place several procedural appeals to various groups to assure the application of sound, sober judgment.

I added psychological assistance to the benefits package. I believe it is essential to understand that "life happens", and the company should be there to support people in times of trouble. Rather than dismiss people for personal problems.

I believe the company benefits from the efforts of every employee. Every employee should benefit from the company.

I believe the people in a company are the company's single most important asset!

It's all about the people!

9 781804 395929